T0243794

'This book could not be more timely as the world grapples with what the post-pandemic workplace should look like. Jeremy Myerson and Philip Ross give us a scholarly yet deeply engaging account of the past, present and future shape of the office. Essential reading for those planning the new office environment – and anyone who's going to have to live in it.'

– Rory Cellan-Jones, former BBC News technology correspondent and author of *Always On: Hope and Fear in the Social Smartphone Era*

'A must-read for understanding the forces that influence how we work. Myerson and Ross expertly examine the facets reshaping the office landscape with a view into "What's Next". *Unworking* is an invaluable guide for anyone interested in the workplaces needed to help people thrive.'

– Harald Becker, Director of Customer Engagements and Insights, Microsoft

'The pandemic has dramatically changed the way we work and how we work. *Unworking* is a fantastic and highly readable book, providing a pathway for the new world of work and the office environments of the future. This is a "must read" for senior executives and many others in navigating the opportunities for future workplaces – you won't regret it!'

– Sir Cary Cooper CBE, 50th Anniversary Professor of Organizational Psychology and Health, University of Manchester

'Brimming with ideas, insights, examples and wisdom, this is the go-to book for everyone interested in the future of the office and curious about the future development of work.'

– Lynda Gratton, Professor of Management Practice, London Business School, and best-selling author of *Redesigning Work*

'To challenge the status quo so that new thinking can emerge, we have to be able to hold both a strong grasp of how we got here, and a deep understanding of the forces that are driving the need for change. Philip Ross and Jeremy Myerson have a wealth of experience and insight in both these areas. They are also consummate communicators: their manifesto is unputdownable, at turns scary and exhilarating, a thrilling invitation to create work – and workspaces – that work for all.'

– David Firth, consultant, coach and author in Organizational Development

'Philip Ross and Jeremy Myerson capture the most significant changes in the world of the office for decades. Their understanding of the social, economic, technology changes and the roles of home and office is unsurpassed.'

– Sir Stuart Lipton, Lipton Rogers Developments

'This compelling, well-written book provides a historical perspective on the world of work, as well as a forward-thinking outlook on how to navigate its impact on our lives. Leisure and work are evermore intertwined, and *Unworking* gave me moments of insight that I can act upon both at work and in private. A joy to read.'

– Cees de Bont, Dean of the School of Design and Creative Arts, Loughborough University

'*Unworking* takes you on panoramic journey, arriving at a plausible, evidence-based future of how work and the workplace will evolve. Rigorous and readable, it offers a better understanding of how we can reinvent the workplace taxonomy.'

– Alessandro Ranaldi, Head of Workplace Consultancy, Foster + Partners

UNWORKING

The Reinvention of the Modern Office

Jeremy Myerson and Philip Ross

REAKTION BOOKS

For Katy, Ollie and Josh
For Wendy, Matthew and Nathan

The future is more exciting than the past

Published by
Reaktion Books Ltd
Unit 32, Waterside
44–48 Wharf Road
London N1 7UX, UK

www.reaktionbooks.co.uk

First published 2022

Printed and bound in Great Britain by TJ Books Ltd, Padstow, Cornwall

A catalogue record for this book is available from the British Library

ISBN 978 1 78914 668 4

Contents

Easter Sunday crowd on Fifth Avenue, New York City, *c.* 1925. The modern office emerged as a central part of city life in the 1920s.

Introduction: Unlearning

If you were to step back into the working world of one hundred years ago, you would see the modern office in full swing. All the pieces were in place, the whole show was in town, whether that town was New York, Chicago or London. Against a background of rapid urbanization, the early 1920s brought together key elements of office life: the industrial technologies of the typewriter, telephone, light bulb, telegraph, vertical filing cabinet and adding machine that enabled vast bureaucracies to process information for set hours, under the steely gaze of time-and-motion supervisors; the tall buildings with fast elevators that reshaped the cityscape as real-estate prices sky-rocketed; the designer-modernist and engineer-management theories that signalled speed, efficiency and progress; the new transport systems above and below ground that ferried people to their places of work from further and further afield.

Today, a century later, our working world presents clear similarities. Against a background of hyper-urbanization, people have been crowding onto public transport systems and clogging up motorways, suburban freeways and city-centre streets trying to get to and from work within set, synchronous hours. More tall buildings than ever litter our skylines, although some have been rebranded 'vertical villages'. A small set of dominant technologies – digital now rather than industrial and analogue – continues to occupy the workforce. Efficiency theory remains surprisingly durable among business managers, and the wheels of the economic growth model continue to turn, albeit in stop-start motion as a series of crises shock the system, the COVID-19 pandemic the most serious among them. On the face of it at least, one could be excused for asking: what has really changed?

Yet behind the eerily familiar facades of our working infrastructure, the modern office, as forged in the crucible of the early twentieth century, is fast being dismantled and reassembled in all its principal parts. We are witnessing the 'swan syndrome' in workplace change: what looked on the surface to be a smooth evolution of the working practices, technologies and ideas first implemented one hundred years ago is, below the waterline, a deep disruption to our way of working – and we're paddling like crazy to keep up as the modern office is completely reinvented. Some of this reinvention can be traced to industrial obsolescence, new theoretical knowledge or changing management fads in a field prone to faddishness. But a significant part of it, especially in the two decades since 2000, can also be attributed to economic shocks, such as the global banking crisis of 2008, environmental shocks, such as the ongoing climate change emergency, and the public health shock of COVID-19, which sent the world's major cities into extended lockdown in 2020, instigating a giant involuntary experiment in remote working, the effects of which are still being played out.

In absorbing these shocks, it is evident that the people who own, plan, build, design, manage, supply, invest in and occupy our offices are being required to relearn pretty much everything they thought they knew about the working world. As we readjust and redefine the new world of work, this unlearning and relearning of the modern office in all its facets is the subject of this book.

IT WAS THE American writer Tom Wolfe who predicted that cities of the early twenty-first century would exactly resemble the cities of 1927. In an essay for the *American Spectator* in December 1987, he claimed that 'the twenty-first century will have a retrograde look and a retrograde mental atmosphere.' People, he said, will look back aghast at a century in which technology leapt forward with such brutal speed and capacity for disaster. That essay was called 'The Great Relearning' and, in it, Wolfe described a process of starting from zero that was evident in many fields. He referenced the year-zero approach of the San Francisco hippy movement of the 1960s to the laws of personal hygiene, for example, which resulted in diseases not seen by medics for centuries – 'the mange, the grunge, the itch, the twitch, the thrush, the scroff, the rot'. Wolfe referenced too the year-zero approach of the Bauhaus design movement, begun in the 1920s, which sought to free us from the dead hand of bourgeois architecture but instead gave us 'the tiny bare beige office cubicles that made workers feel like component parts'.

If the modern office was itself originally propelled by the year-zero thinking of the industrial management era in the early twentieth century, it is now in the process of returning to first principles to reimagine what our workplaces might become. This unlearning is everywhere we look in the world of work and the workplace today. Office planning and design took its early cues in the 1920s from the machine, only later significantly adapting this model under the influence of social democracy and digital technology. Office planning and design used to be primarily about what people do at work; today, it's all about what they *feel* about work. The psychological experience of employees barely rated any consideration in the age of efficiency – now the experiential dimension of work is everywhere. The office used to be an extension of the factory floor, functional and utilitarian; now it is being recast as the sentient workplace.

This book traces the development of the modern office. In Chapters One, Two and Three, in the section titled 'The Journey to Now', we explore how we've arrived at where we are today, by explaining what formed and informed the office and the rhythm of working life, the cityscape and our experience of commuting; the chapters also survey the courage of the mould-breakers and the emergence of new ideas driven by the coworking movement. No one predicted the global pandemic and with it the reappraisal of work and the workplace, together with the constraints imposed by governments and authorities on movement, interaction and proximity. But COVID-19's arrival coincided with a number of broad forces that were already challenging the status quo and reshaping our ideas about the future of work.

There are ten forces or facets at play in reshaping the landscape, each examined in the section 'What Comes Next'. From the very essence of an organization, through disruption driven by digital change, to the expectations and aspirations of people navigating the post-pandemic world of work, a new vision to reinvent the modern office is taking shape. As we explain in Chapter Four, a shift from work processes to subjective experience is forcing building owners, landlords and employers, who have rarely given a jot about how the occupiers of offices feel, to consider new amenities to address employee psychology. It is also forcing some rewiring of organizational structures, as the powerful departmental silos of HR (dealing with people), facilities management (space) and IT (technology) are now compelled to collaborate properly for the first time – or even disband in favour of offering a single, unified service – in order to deliver a more satisfactory working day to employees at every level.

Office buildings were once dumb containers for work, oblivious to who or what was going on inside their walls. Today, these buildings are becoming smart – so much so that they are increasingly able to use digital technology to track occupancy, predictively adapt environmental conditions and mould experience. Office buildings were constructed to portray the stability, permanence and predictability of the organization. Today, as we discuss in Chapter Five, they bear witness to dynamic, unpredictable, non-repeating patterns of work. Companies are starting to dismantle their inflexible, fixed hierarchies in favour of more fluid and agile management structures. Organizational theory is alive with new ideas.

The leadership of companies inside office buildings used to be rigid and hierarchical, based on command-and-control structures and often requiring visible line of sight of employees present at work. Today, such models appear outdated. Leaderships styles are evolving. Agile teams, adaptive systems, distributed working and self-organizing groups are rewriting the rules of management.

It isn't just that buildings or organizations are changing. The cities they so aggressively shape have begun to change too, as we see in Chapter Six. Central business districts, so dominant for so long, are slowly being relocated and reimagined as smart precincts or innovation districts. These new quarters have mixed-use characteristics and an unprecedented permeability to broader city life, and are often clustered in a new way around transport nodes, universities or shopping centres. In the 2020s, we're in an age of tactical urbanism every bit as restless and improvisatory as the boom-and-bust office years of the 1920s, but with different objectives in mind.

Approaches to interior space are changing as well. People inside offices used to be mainly static and sedentary at their desks; now they are becoming more agile and mobile both within and beyond the building, as the technologies that tied us to the desk are giving way to ones that free us from it. Chapter Seven explores these changes and also considers the home, a place that used to offer a domestic retreat or sanctuary from work but has now become an extension of the workspace itself, especially in the aftermath of the global pandemic.

Indeed, the old demarcations between home, leisure and work are dissolving. If the office was once a machine for working – an extension of the architect Le Corbusier's idea of the house as a machine for living – its conceptual model is no longer based on hard engineering metaphors but on soft biomorphic ones instead. People used to be marooned at a desk deep within an interior, miles from a window; now workspaces are filled with light and air, as well as sofas, plants, high-end coffee machines, open kitchens, ice-cream kiosks, music rooms and much else besides.

Underpinning all the profound changes to our workspaces, buildings, organizations and urban districts is the relentless impact of digital technology (see Chapter Eight). The modern office of the past hundred years was driven by people working with physical artefacts and systems housed on-site – today the entire infrastructure of work is disappearing into 'the cloud'. A new data-led workplace is starting to emerge as part of a continuum of digital work across time, place and space. Smartphones, sensors and apps are the twenty-first-century equivalent of stopwatches, desks and metal filing cabinets stuffed with paper.

For office designers, the formulaic approaches, the bland 'vanilla' solutions and the universal plans that dominated for so long are being abandoned in favour of variety and eclecticism based on a more human-centric and individualistic design credo. One size no longer fits all. Even the process of designing offices is being transformed. Workplace design once relied heavily on interpreting a management brief and studying the 'org' chart, which set out the organization like an electrical diagram.

Today, as we explore in Chapter Nine, the use of data science and generative design with algorithms is changing the picture. Office workers, who rarely had a voice in the past, are being invited to participate in designing their own space.

The things that made people the same drove the planning of the modern office – now we seek to identify what makes people different and plan around that instead. Diversity was suppressed for a long time amid the homogeneity of the modernist template; now it is beginning to be prized in all its forms. In this kaleidoscope of change, surveyed in Chapter Ten, we find a wider mix of age, gender, ability, ethnicity and culture in the office workforce. We find too a growing acceptance that a more diverse workforce is better equipped to address the innovation challenges of the knowledge economy by spotting patterns and using imagination outside of typical boundaries.

If the productivity-obsessed modern office of the twentieth century gave any thought to the health and well-being of its workers, this was simply to keep the cogs in the machine running. Today there is an unprecedented interest in workplace well-being, as we will see in Chapter Eleven, especially in relation to concerns around mental health, and a growing number of innovative ways to address it. The traditional office was a singular concept – closed off from the outside world and single-minded in character. Today, it is becoming a more hybrid and permeable environment. This hybridity, as we'll explore in Chapter Twelve, takes many forms – not just hybrid work that balances office and home but mixed-use developments and workplaces in which humans and robots share the same space. Indeed, the rise of automation and artificial intelligence asks new questions about our future workplace.

The mid-twentieth-century office was aimed at what economists call 'the family-formation workforce' of 21- to 45-year-olds, overwhelmingly white, able-bodied and male. Today the demography of the workplace, discussed in Chapter Thirteen, presents a different picture. It is bookended by older workers, who are not yet at the age of retirement and still have plenty to offer, and Generation Z entrants, whose digital habits, values and preferences are set to radically shake up how we will work in the future.

Everywhere you look today in the world of work, up is down, black is white, square is round, home is work, work is home. As we see in Chapter Fourteen, the shocks of the global pandemic are reverberating through the system but are often accelerating pre-existing trends as much as disrupting them. A 'slow work' movement linked to mindfulness is disrupting a century-long obsession with speed and efficiency. Even going to an office no longer has the same purpose: there is an expectation of human buzz, social connection and shared creative endeavour, not a quiet environment to get your head down and get things done. Economic value as the prime motivator is being challenged by activist employees who want to generate social value and help shape a new type of capitalism. We had blue collar, then white collar, now we have no collar.

The modern office – as fully revealed to the world a century ago – has sought to contain this sweeping tide of contradictions and reversals but, under unprecedented strain, it is now shifting to a series of new positions. Describing and critiquing what these new positions might be is the central objective of this book. Our term 'unworking' describes the process by which we might unbundle the old assumptions that are baked into the modern office and unlearn the working habits, management styles and cultures that are so ingrained in us. In Chapter Fifteen, we sketch out a future workplace that is more social, sustainable, sentient, elastic, fluid and personalized, reinventing the modern office with a mix of digital technologies, design practices and organizational strategies.

WHAT GIVES US the right to pronounce on the future of work? The shifts we discuss here have unfolded right before our eyes. Indeed, we gave ourselves the best possible ringside seats to witness the reinvention of the modern office over the past twenty years or so. In 2003, we launched a conference called Worktech with the British Library in London, which sought to look at the future of work and the workplace in a more holistic way. We wanted to create a forum to generate new ideas and showcase best practice that considered people, place and technology in the round. We were tired of attending events that either cast the future of work around technical devices and gadgets or reduced the subject to a matter of architectural facades, furniture and finishes. We wanted human behaviour and human sciences to be part of the story. We needed data and evidence. We wanted to look at who was innovating in the field and not just sticking to an established formula.

The Worktech conference started slowly but soon became a fixture in thirty cities around the world – from New York, Sydney, Singapore and San Francisco to Tokyo, Berlin, Hong Kong, Amsterdam, Munich, Copenhagen, Toronto and Geneva, as well as across Latin America and India. Worktech's worldwide reach enabled us to get a sense of emerging global trends in the field. Twelve years after we launched the event series, we established Worktech Academy, an online knowledge platform and membership club, to capture and share the insights and evidence emanating from the conference and its professional network. The Academy acts as a bridge between new research and practice on the ground.

Over the years, more than 2,000 leading speakers – business leaders, innovators, authors, architects, entrepreneurs, technologists, HR specialists, academics, scientists and real-estate practitioners of all stripes – have spoken at Worktech. The predictions, models and ideas they have shared with conference audiences essentially describe the 'great unlearning' of the workplace and form the basis of this book, whose title flips the central mission of the modern office – working – on its head.

Back in 1925, W. H. Leffingwell, a disciple of the time-and motion experiments of Frederick Taylor, published *Office Management Principles and Practice*. This was widely regarded as the bible of office efficiency and was conceived to be the last word on a serious subject. But neither Leffingwell nor Taylor could scarcely have imagined that less than a century later, office executives in Silicon Valley would spend their hours at serious play making ducks out of Lego bricks, as memorably chronicled by Dan Lyons in his 2018 book *Lab Rats*.

To work out how the modern office went from the sternly mechanistic world of Leffingwell to Lyons's life on a California campus or in a Boston start-up with their faux European cafés, all-day snacking, table tennis, Fearless Fridays for team-building, agile methodologies and colourful innovation playpens, first we need to retrace our steps and go on a journey from 1920 to now. If we want to see the future, we must understand the past.

PART I

THE JOURNEY TO NOW

Interior of the Union Carbide Building on Park Avenue, New York, 1960. Designed by architects Skidmore, Owings & Merrill, its mechanical componentry captured the essence of the efficiency-driven modern office.

1 Efficiency

If the daily grind of the clock-watching workers inside the city-centre office buildings of the early 1920s was a world away from the yoga classes and juice bars inside some of today's workplaces, it was also a world away from the genteel life of the nineteenth-century clerking class just a few short decades before. The technical accomplishments of the new era signalled a decisive break with a thousand-year continuum of human-scale work in which people worked either alone or with a handful of colleagues in smallish, easily negotiable spaces. Is it possible to imagine how an office clerk from the Dickensian era, seated at his comfortable roll-top desk in the mid-nineteenth century, would have felt had he looked up suddenly from his ledger and found himself transported into the giant machinery of the modern office of 1920?

In his book *Cubed: A Secret History of the Workplace*, writer and sociologist Nikil Saval tries exactly that thought experiment, describing it thus:

> He might have been surprised to see that his familiar small surroundings had melted away entirely, converted into a

> space whose high ceilings and tall columns resembled nothing so much as a cave swollen with stalactites. His lone colleague and brother-in-arms, the clerk, was gone, replaced by dozens of unfamiliar faces surrounding him in neat serried rows of desks. The cigar-chomping partner at the nearby rolltop desk would be gone too, having multiplied into a small squadron of bosses locked in snug executive suites high up in the stratosphere.[1]

Saval describes the shock of the new in 1920:

> His work is now harried, insistent, relentless. Farewell the tranquil, languorous days of the countinghouse; greetings to the factory-like labor of the office . . . Men with stopwatches record the motions of his pencil, his filing habits, when and whether he goes to the bathroom, how long he lingers at the watercooler, how many minutes he wastes.

The new office, Saval goes on to explain, came with its own sounds and rituals:

> the high-pitched metal clack of the typewriter, the adding machine, the sliding and slamming of cabinet. He clocks in and out; shrill bells ring in his workday and push him out into the early evening darkness, shoved and jostled by the black-coated thousands following him, out of his office, in an endless dark stream.[2]

Design historian Adrian Forty describes the disorientation of the individual late nineteenth-century office clerk in less poetic terms. In his book *Objects of Desire* (1986), he explains how the clerk's comfortable status was eroded first by the division of labour and then by the emerging field of scientific management. Furniture design played a key role in this. The standard nineteenth-century office desk – ornamental, designed to store papers and indicative of a master in charge of his own domain – was gradually replaced by a modern design dedicated only to shifting papers as swiftly as possible. Chairs were altered too. Forty explains: 'The new design signified the change in the nature of clerical work. Taking away the high back meant that the clerk no longer worked in a private space: the chief clerk or supervisor was able to see whether he or she was working at maximum efficiency.'[3]

The pursuit of efficiency, with managers removing personal autonomy and controlling all aspects of the work process, lay at the heart of every design decision in the modern office. 'The inescapable reality was that efficiency was the ultimate aim of the office,' observes Forty. This played out fully in the development of the workplace. According to Jennifer Kaufmann-Buhler, author of *Open Plan: A Design History of the American Office* (2021), the 'plan' aspect of open plan provides 'a system of order, control, and power that disciplines the space, the organization, and the worker'.[4] By the 1920s, efficiency shone through the office like letters through a stick of rock. It was the main consideration behind the selection of every design for every aspect, from furniture to facades and floor layouts, reflecting the emergence of the modern clerical workplace as an administrative adjunct of the factory and harking back to the dawn of the Industrial Revolution.

IF EFFICIENCY SWIFTLY became the driving force of the modern office – and remained its lifeblood for the next hundred years – where did this philosophy emanate from? The story of the emergence of the modern office coincides with the production-line innovations of Fordism, but most experts point the finger not at Henry Ford but at another pivotal figure: the American engineer Frederick Taylor (1856–1915), a pioneer of early workflow experiments in time and motion who adapted factory principles to the white-collar workplace with ruthless efficiency.[5]

Frederick Taylor was obsessed with the measurement of human performance of all kinds. Nikil Saval's assessment of him is cold-eyed: 'Less generous observers might have called him a maniac.'[6] Taylor's overriding view was that there was not a single worker 'who does not devote a considerable part of his time to studying just how slowly he can work and still convince his employer that he is going at a good pace'.[7] He believed that 'in the past man has been first. In the future, the system must be first.' Taylor was opposed to the union organization of labour, then springing up in the new paper factories, and his ideas about scientific management were held up in American business schools such as Harvard and Wharton as the means to crush trade union syndicalism and compete on more equal terms with the British Empire.

Taylor's ideology peaked around 1911, the 'year of efficiency'. A profile in the *New-York Tribune* appeared under the heading 'Weeding Waste Out of Business Is This Man's Special Joy'.[8] Taylor wrote that the analysis of any piece of work into its elements 'always reveals the fact that many of the conditions surrounding and accompanying the work are defective. Knowledge so obtained leads frequently to constructive work of a high order, to the standardization of tools and conditions, to the invention of superior methods and machines.' In 1911, four years before his death from pneumonia, Taylor consolidated his ideas in a book, *The Principles of Scientific Management*. This argued that adoption of new methods, conditions and standards needed to be 'enforced' by management.

By the 1920s, Taylorism, named after its puritanical creator, had not only matured and endured, but was set to persist for decades to come. Scientific management principles, which viewed the workplace as a rational system of production and adopted design characteristics suited to the dominant economic model, influenced Imperial Japan, Nazi Germany and the rapidly industrializing Soviet Union. Lenin's critique of Taylorism is revealing: 'The Taylor system . . . like all capitalist progress, is a combination of the refined brutality of the bourgeois system and a number of the greatest scientific achievements in the field of analysing mechanical motions during work.'[9]

Taylorism gave the modern office its greatest governing metaphor – the workplace as a machine, comprised of many moving industrial parts, with the human element either massively

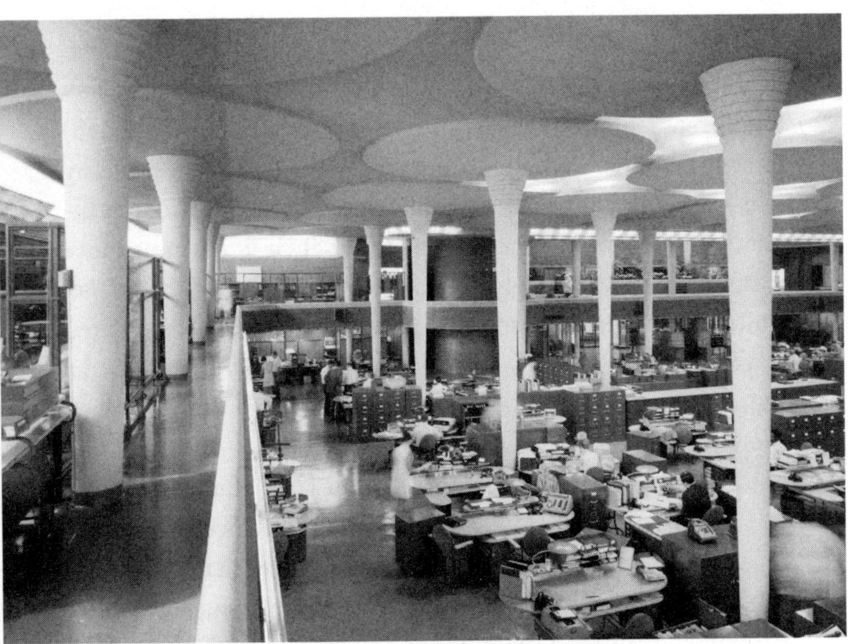

Interior of the Johnson Wax Corporation Building, designed by Frank Lloyd Wright and completed in 1939: a high-design interpretation of scientific management.

mistrusted or completely overlooked. Taylorism also bequeathed the organizational diagram (or 'org chart') that presented the hierarchies and reporting lines of the company as an electric circuit board with complicated wiring. As a legacy of Frederick Taylor, the challenge of organizational work for most of the twentieth century thus became all about solving an engineering puzzle. And as management efficiency theory advocated an ever-tightening grip on office employees (cogs in the machine, literally), so modernist, machine-age design was on hand to mirror this approach in hard-edged, rectilinear form.

Modern design pre-dated the international clamour for Taylorism. Frank Lloyd Wright's Larkin Building in Buffalo, New York, designed in 1904, is widely cited as the first iconic project of the modern office: its vast atrium space proclaimed the unity of the organization and the power of the business owner, with the corporate slogan 'Intelligence, Enthusiasm, Control' emblazoned on the walls. Beneath these words, mail-order company employees laboured in total silence (conversation was banned) in serried ranks under close supervision. The Larkin Building was even sited next to a railway station to make it more efficient for workers to commute. However, it is perhaps more instructive to look closely at Frank Lloyd Wright's Johnson Wax Building in Racine, Wisconsin, constructed 1936–9, completed 25 years after 'efficiency fever' first took hold. This presented a more sophisticated take on scientific management and was even more rigid in its expression of Taylor's ideas.

By the 1940s, the great Bauhaus 'white gods' of modern architecture, as writer Tom Wolfe described them, were leaving Europe, crossing the Atlantic and making their presence felt in U.S. design schools and corporate firms. Modernist pioneers such as Walter Gropius and Mies van der Rohe had honed their new International Style amid the radical politics and worker housing of 1920s Weimar Germany. Now, ironically, they assumed positions of

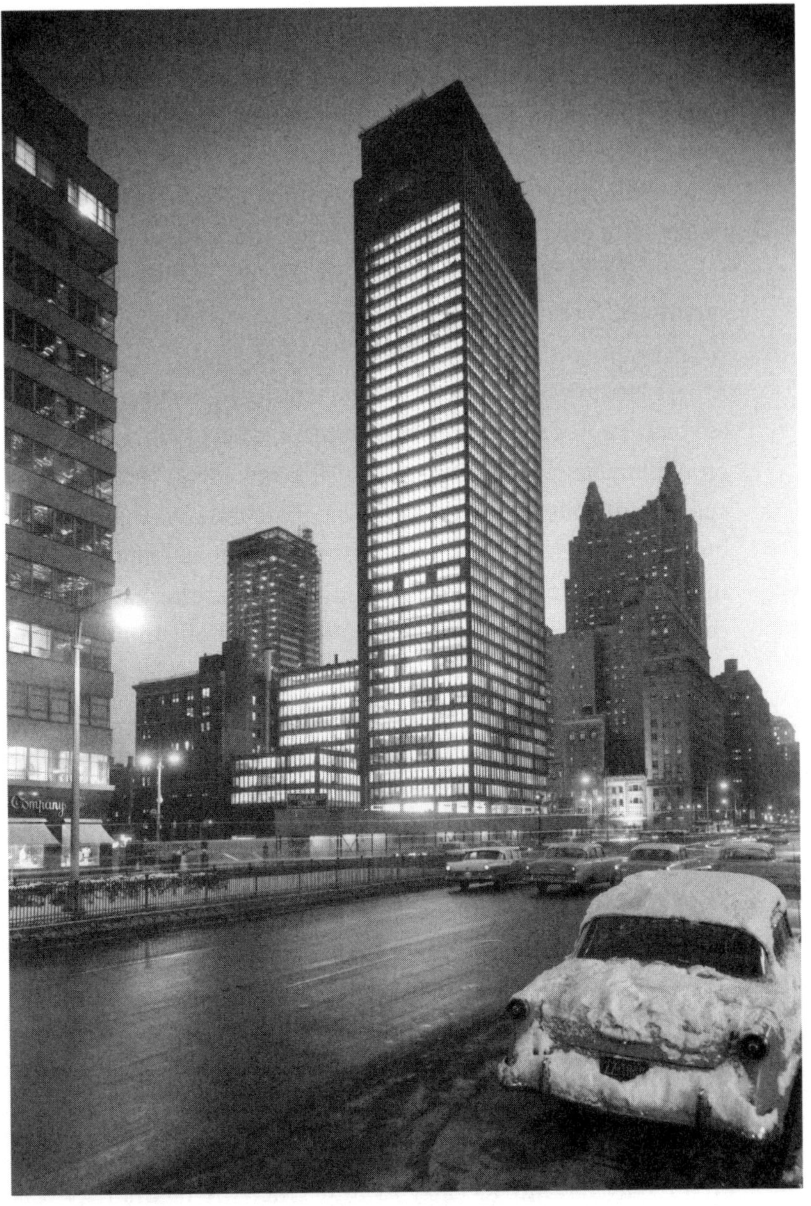

The Seagram Building, 1958, in New York. Originally the headquarters for a Canadian distiller but better known as the workplace totem of the modern movement, designed by Ludwig Mies van der Rohe and Philip Johnson.

authority in the design professions serving U.S. business. The symbolic value of the modern office to the cause of the Modern movement was not lost on Le Corbusier, who wrote in *Towards a New Architecture* (1923): 'Our modern life . . . has created its own objects; its own costume, its own fountain pen, its eversharp pencil, its typewriter, its telephone, its admirable office furniture.'[10]

AFTER THE SECOND WORLD WAR, technical developments such as steel-framed structures in architecture led to office buildings on expensive city-centre sites with large, clear, lettable floor spaces unhindered by columns or obstructions. Inside these buildings, Taylorism continued as the dominant model. Office interiors resembled a machine in their modular assembly of component parts. Desks were carefully laid out in rectilinear patterns. Clerical staff toiled inside large bull pens within the deep space while more senior executives were given, progressively, window access, perimeter offices, larger desks, more domesticated furniture (usually in wood), artworks and private dining rooms as they moved up through the command-and-control ranks. As Jennifer Kaufmann-Buhler explains, 'the process of designing new corporate buildings in the mid-twentieth century with newly defined space standards created a fresh interpretation of the rationalized and standardized organizational hierarchy.'[11]

In this new world of strange bedfellows, the ideologies of modern design and management efficiency became twinned. Mies van der Rohe had envisaged a towering glass office block on a triangular site as early as 1919. Once the technology was available, he realized his aims with the Seagram Building, New York, in 1958. This building and the nearby Union Carbide tower on Park Avenue, designed a year later by Skidmore, Owings & Merrill, with an imposing architectural grid to support lighting,

The Apartment, directed by Billy Wilder in 1960, told a dark story of desperation in the hierarchical corporate workplace.

air conditioning and partitions in a machine-like interior, set the template for office design for several decades.

By this time, popular culture was absorbing the deep shock of the reality of the modern office and a backlash was overdue. Billy Wilder's classic 1960 film *The Apartment* features a junior clerk, played by Jack Lemmon, who ingratiates himself with senior managers in a bid to escape the office-factory floor and gain a key to the executive washroom. The scientifically managed office was exaggerated – but not by much. In fact, the entire film, including its long opening sequence of endless streams of office workers, was an elaborate homage to King Vidor's 1928 film *The Crowd*, itself a stark polemic against the dehumanizing aspects of regimented office life in the 1920s. Jacques Tati's blackly humorous 1967 French movie *Playtime* went further than any before in depicting the Taylorist office as a bureaucratic nightmare of Kafkaesque proportions.

Jacques Tati's cinematic tour de force *Playtime* (1967) took the strange banality of the modern office to the heart of popular culture.

Even progressive thinkers in the field like Robert Propst, who designed Action Office for Herman Miller in 1964, were destined to be thwarted by such a powerful model. Action Office was a furniture system designed to encourage movement and sharing in the coming age of knowledge work rather than keeping the clerical worker in their place. But its set of anonymous industrial componentry was misunderstood and misused, and the resulting dehumanizing effect was criticized. Despite its good intentions, Action Office eventually led to the rise of the detested office cubicle – one of the prominent markers of efficiency gone mad.

The trouble was that in giving managers complete control over the office environment, the balance between organizational and individual needs was twisted out of alignment. By the 1980s, termed a 'decade of corporate efficiency', a slew of new

Herman Miller's Action Office furniture system designed by Robert Probst, 1964. A high-minded project that morphed into the modular office cubicle.

technologies tightened the screw further.[12] The workplace was streamlined ruthlessly to meet business objectives. High-speed lifts and controlled environments with computerized lighting and centralized air conditioning took away individual control in the pursuit of the so-called intelligent building. Word processors gave way to the networked personal computer that tethered people to their desks and created the need to accommodate miles of structured cabling that snaked its way round the building, through furniture and raised floors. Clear, unobstructed sight-lines reinforced supervision. People seated deep inside large city-centre blocks no longer recognized if it was day or night, or what the temperature was outside. These were things that not even Frederick Taylor had denied the office clerk seventy years before.

Inevitably, this efficiency-first focus affected human well-being. Environmental researchers began to identify something called 'sick building syndrome' – flu-like symptoms of lethargy, stuffiness and headaches caused by oppressive conditions. Lack of individual control was cited as a major contributory factor. Managers and designers began the delicate task of loosening the nuts on the engineering puzzle, exploring new ways to make the work environment more flexible and human. The action switched from super-efficient buildings to more agile interior settings. The British workplace design pioneer Frank Duffy described 'a massive emigration of problem-solving from the realms of architecture into that of office furnishings'.[13] It made more economic sense to invest in autonomous elements that could be reconfigured rather than a fixed building shell which couldn't be changed.

In the search for productivity, companies started to look not only at reconfigurable work interiors but at other ways to offer employees less stressful, more comfortable and more flexible working conditions, thus mitigating the worst effects of efficiency theory. By the new millennium, Duffy's team at the architects and planners DEGW talked about moving the office design story on from efficiency to effectiveness and expression.[14] Part of this was an emphasis on community, which we will come to. However, it is impossible to overstate the central importance of efficiency to the evolution of the modern office. Even today it hangs over our world of work like a black cloud, defying new models of management to relax its iron grip.

2 Community

In January 1988, Scandinavia's largest airline, SAS, moved into large and airy new headquarters at Frösundavik, just outside Stockholm. Designed by Norwegian architect Niels Torp, this building completely refashioned the traditional concept of office life as an efficiency machine. An entire community was created with shops, restaurants and coffee bars lining a solar-heated internal 'main street' that ran down the spine of an enormous glazed structure before opening out onto a lakeside restaurant. SAS president Jan Carlzon was justifiably proud of this expansive new concept and he encouraged senior SAS managers to promenade up and down the 'street' in order to meet staff informally, in a social context, to generate and monitor projects.

The only trouble was that as he ambled up and down the central boulevard, Carlzon realized that very few of his employees felt they had permission to take a stroll too. The place was deserted. So he sent an all-staff memo instructing SAS employees to leave their desks and show up in the street at least once a day. Carlzon championed the new approach with a vigorous defence of multi-purpose public space in the office. He argued:

SAS building, Stockholm, designed in 1988 by Norwegian architect Niels Torp. The solar-lit central street signalled the zenith of the social democratic office.

> A service company cannot be a hierarchy, and it would be absurd for us to have a chateau with rampart and towers for our head office . . . Good ideas are rarely created when you are sitting at your desk feeling alone and tense, but during creative encounters between human beings . . . Meeting a colleague from another department for a coffee is not the same as shirking your duties.[1]

Carlzon's approach was summarized in his seminal 1985 book *Moments of Truth*, which described the importance of touchpoints where customers come into contact with an organization and form an impression. Carlzon recognized the importance of interaction and the empowerment of workers to provide better customer service. That Carlzon had to give permission for people to take a coffee break with a colleague in plain sight is revealing, but SAS at Frösundavik was reversing seventy-odd years of Taylorist office working at a stroke. The new HQ was as far away from Taylorism in aesthetic and organizational terms as you could get: a city of its own on the outskirts of a city, with a swimming pool, a medical centre and a gym, park benches, cafés and a conference centre. It reflected the need to provide every kind of social amenity for large numbers of workers no longer based in the centre of cities but transported to edge-of-town business parks and marooned in the middle of nowhere. It did much more than that, however: it gave the purest of forms to a social democratic ideal for the workplace and its influence was destined to stretch far beyond Scandinavia.

Architects from all over the world studied Niels Torp's building closely, and several of its innovations worked their way into British, German and American offices. Multinationals were particularly enamoured of the community-based approach with its public routes, plazas, greenery and water features, giving desk-based workers a break for informal and spontaneous social interaction. British Airways was not content to absorb only some aspects of Torp's template; it directly commissioned the architect to replicate the SAS project at Heathrow Airport, with the Waterside building. This was completed in 1998 at a cost of £200 million. In its scale and expense, Waterside represented a high watermark for the social democratic office in the UK. With its leafy views for all employees from narrow, finger-like building wings attached to a central spine, it served as a rebuke to offices which had grown so large and fat that people toiled in cubicles far from a view of outside.

The SAS building outside Stockholm didn't happen out of nowhere. It reflected wider developments in Europe since the end of the Second World War. The social democratic or community office grew out of the darkness of fascism and a determination to rebuild Europe's shattered economies brighter and better in the years after 1945. This new approach to the office was less preoccupied with the raw economics of efficiency and was often modelled for social dynamics on the layout of a village or main street.

As an organizational model, it departed decisively from the Taylorist office in many ways. It placed growing importance on human factors and informal social networks to make work happen, rather than on fixed hierarchies and time-and-motion. Its most pioneering projects reflected the rising power of the white-collar unions in northern Europe and Scandinavia, whereas Taylorism had been seen in the USA as a way to beat down the unions. The community workplace was pioneered by owner-occupiers investing in purpose-built 'cathedrals of commerce' for the longer term; this was in stark contrast to many property developers who surfed the Taylorist wave by leasing their efficient buildings to corporate tenants.

The Taylorist offices of the 1920s had been essentially an adjunct of the factory; as the twentieth century progressed there was a gradual separation between factory and office conditions. The social democratic office that took shape in the 1950s and '60s was the clearest expression of this progression. In this era of relatively full employment, office-based employers competed with factories and mines for staff not by paying higher wages, but simply by offering more respectable and pleasant surroundings that acknowledged the need for social exchange and interaction.[2]

The first real expression of this new approach came from the Quickborner consulting team in Germany, which pioneered the concept of *Bürolandschaft* (office landscaping) in the late 1950s. Quickborner was formed by two brothers, Wolfgang and Eberhard Schnelle, who worked as assistants at their father's Hamburg furniture company. Sensing an opportunity amid the dull uniformity of the period, they decided to divide up the office layout not into regimented rows of desks, which Taylor's time-and-motion studies had encouraged, but in a way that treated the workspace as an organic whole. Rigid, rectangular space-planning evident in the USA gave way to more open, flowing lines, based on analyses of work communication, that were supposed to increase a sense of democracy and community in the office.

This represented a significant step forward in office design, and European firms were fast to pick up on the more engaging and flexible spaces of *Bürolandschaft*. Early sample office layouts produced by the Schnelle brothers in a demo warehouse space seemed unplanned, even chaotic. But, with their informal areas for relaxation and elegant planters, they spoke of the possibilities for the office to escape the image of the machine. By the 1960s, Quickborner had established teams in the UK and the United States, and in 1967 the first American 'office landscape' was designed on a single floor for Du Pont. Corporate America embraced the German import of *Bürolandschaft* just as enthusiastically as it had embraced the imported German modernism

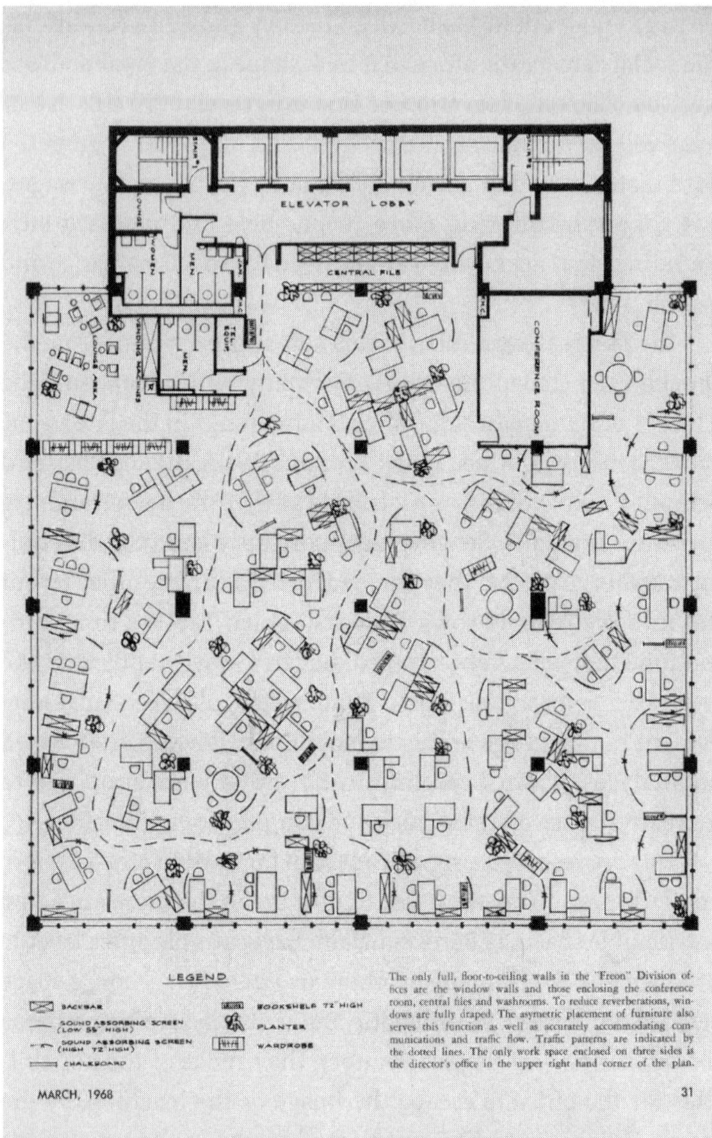

The only full, floor-to-ceiling walls in the "Freon" Division offices are the window walls and those enclosing the conference room, central files and washrooms. To reduce reverberations, windows are fully draped. The asymetric placement of furniture also serves this function as well as accurately accommodating communications and traffic flow. Traffic patterns are indicated by the dotted lines. The only work space enclosed on three sides is the director's office in the upper right hand corner of the plan.

MARCH, 1968 31

Bürolandschaft office layout from the late 1950s by the Quickborner team in Germany: a step towards towards the idea of a dynamic work community.

of the Bauhaus design school. Eastman Kodak, Port Authority of New York and Purdue University were among the organizations that adopted office landscaping.

Bürolandschaft didn't end the hierarchies of the Taylorist office, however; it merely disguised them. Over time, they reasserted themselves (even though desks may have been positioned at an odd angle when compared with previous layouts). Beneath the aesthetic appeal of *Bürolandschaft* to individual communication needs, the office continued to adhere to a mechanistic model, and its furniture accordingly followed a system-based approach. In any history of the workplace, Robert Propst's Action Office for Herman Miller, first developed in 1964, might comfortably fit into either the community or the efficiency narrative around the modern office. *Bürolandschaft* also belonged to a collection of high-design office concepts that were being imposed on workers from above by their bosses. As the design historian Jennifer Kaufmann-Buhler observes: 'Even as the open plan projected an image of greater inclusivity, hierarchy was always an integral part . . . that codified and reinforced the positions, priorities and preferences of those in power.'[3]

BY THE 1970S, the mood was changing across Europe. Unions were becoming more militant; white-collar employees were forming workplace councils to demand more say in their working conditions. Italy, Germany, Sweden and the Netherlands passed laws to put employee representatives on company boards. The social democratic office was about to shift gear. In 1972, the Dutch architect Herman Hertzberger completed the Centraal Beheer insurance building at Apeldoorn in the Netherlands. This project took the idea of the office as community to a new level. Hertzberger's office building for a thousand people comprised 56 cubic elements of 9 metres × 9 metres (30 × 30 ft) located around a core containing lifts, stairs and bathrooms. Seen from above, it was reminiscent of the street pattern of a medieval town.

Inside, Hertzberger created a complex interlocking interior with an ambiguously mounting series of concrete block 'work islands'.[4] Each unit housed around a dozen workers who were free to decorate their team space as they wished with paint, furniture and plants, and even bring their dogs to work (this was Holland, after all). Hertzberger's achievement was hailed as intellectual modernism with a human face, a solution that gave employees both privacy and a sense of belonging to the communal office. Nearly half a century after it was built, the Centraal Beheer insurance building remains as popular with staff as the day it opened.

What Hertzberger started with his complex community geometries, Norwegian architect Niels Torp completed with his sweeping Swedish solar-lit main street. Thus the cast was set for the social democratic office as the default position for the multinational corporations creating, at great cost, their own community-based buildings and campuses. What both landmark projects shared was an interest in social theories of design. The office building was no longer simply a container for workers, structured for maximum operational efficiency, but an enabler and shaper of work, using the plan and its details for broader psychological effect. That seemingly unbreakable alliance between management process and modernist design was called into question for the first time. The office was no longer an engineering puzzle alone: it was a human one, too. By the 1990s, once the practice outliers had been absorbed by the mainstream, many workplace designers stopped looking to the future for inspiration, as the pioneer modernists once did, but to the past.

Architects and their clients explored historical precedents in a bid to learn how tight-knit communities of a few hundred

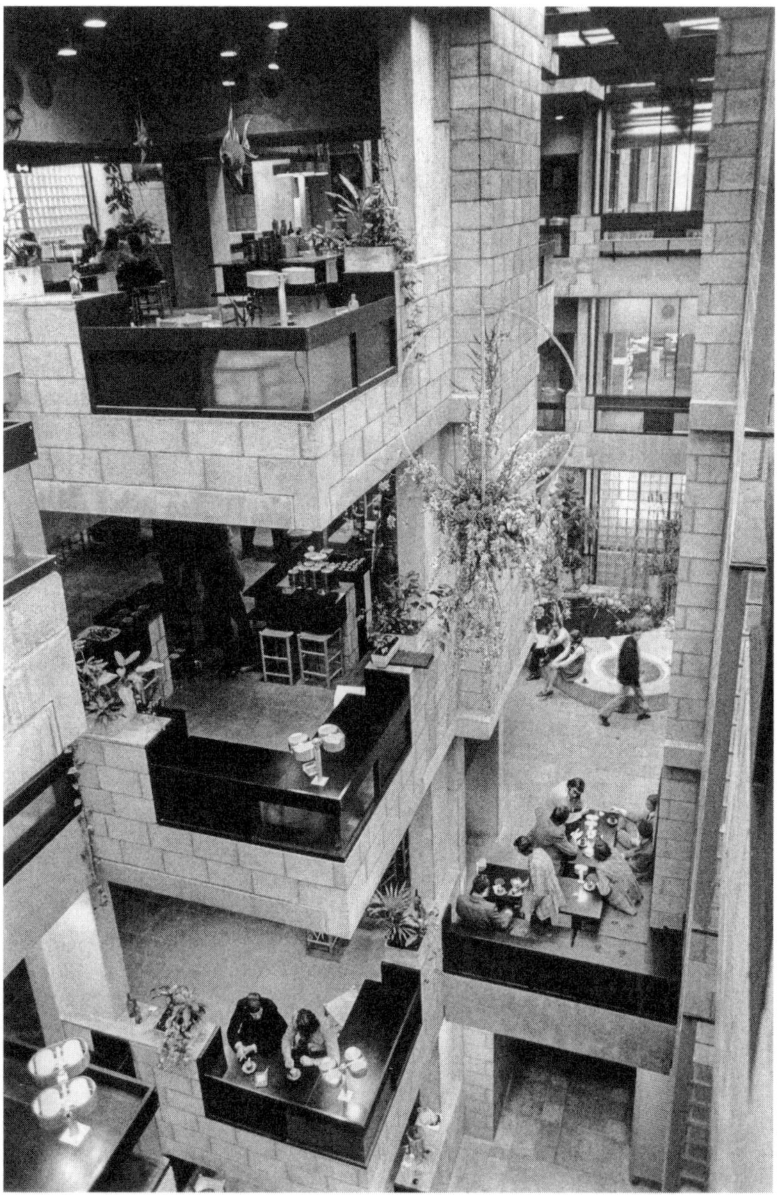

Interior of Centraal Beheer office, Apeldoorn, the Netherlands, 1972. Herman Hertzberger's design encased social democratic principles in concrete blocks.

people could occupy space in a socially cohesive and economically viable way. In a rebuff to year-zero modernism, they studied medieval villages, hilltop settlements and bridge communities. They painstakingly pored over the Greek agora, the North African kasbah, the traditional Oxbridge quad and the Cotswolds craft guild. In the early 1990s an office scheme by Studios Architecture for Babcock & Brown, a U.S. investment bank housed in a former warehouse on the San Francisco waterfront, caught this new mood.[5] On the top floor of the Hills Brothers Building, constructed in 1926 for a coffee trader, the Babcock & Brown office was laid out like the topology of a medieval town, complete with a gatehouse guarding the executive suites and an open space akin to a parvis in front of a cathedral. There were also two raised neighbourhoods styled as 'hilltop' work areas, one accessed by a meandering ramp, the other by a more formal staircase.

The quest to create thriving office-based communities of practice returned time and again to the language of urban planning and landscape architecture. In the process, Jane Jacobs's landmark book on the decline of U.S. neighbourhoods, *The Death and Life of Great American Cities* (1961), was reissued and enjoyed new popularity as a primer for workplace design during the 1990s. Jacobs wrote about the characteristics (and characters) that made neighbourhoods like Greenwich Village such convivial places to live. She analysed how human scale, diversity and mixed use brought districts alive for people. Workplace designers duly took note as they tried to breathe new life into office towers or old warehouses.

When architect Clive Wilkinson relocated the U.S. advertising agency TBWA Chiat Day to a Los Angeles warehouse building in 1998, he recreated an intelligent pastiche of early 1960s Greenwich Village within the plan in a bid to design the ideal creative community for several hundred people. The ground floor was bisected by a tree-lined main street, with staff sharing 'public' amenities

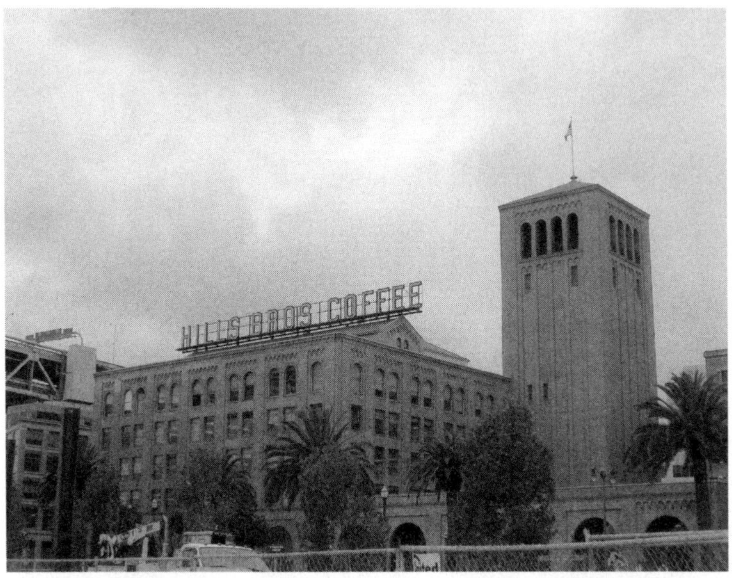

The 1926 Hills Brothers Building in San Francisco, originally built for a coffee company, was revitalized in the early 1990s to house the offices of investment bank Babcock & Brown. Studios Architecture laid out the space on the postmodern principles of a medieval town.

such as a park, a baseball court and cafés. In a second Californian project for another advertising agency three years later, Foote, Cone & Belding, Wilkinson pushed the retro-community template even further by constructing a 'harbour community' in a former factory. The space was divided between an orderly 'landside' area with wooden dockside structures and hanging sailboards facing onto a more random 'sea' of green and blue work desks.

Such elaborate postmodern office metaphors reflect, in historian Eric Hobsbawm's terminology, a 'reinvention of tradition'. But they were more than just presentational: they were designed to face inwards and influence the behaviour and performance of the individuals working in such environments in a new way. So another way to look at such design schemes is as an embodiment of the term 'organizational ecology', first defined in 1981 by Cornell academic Franklin Becker as the interdependence of

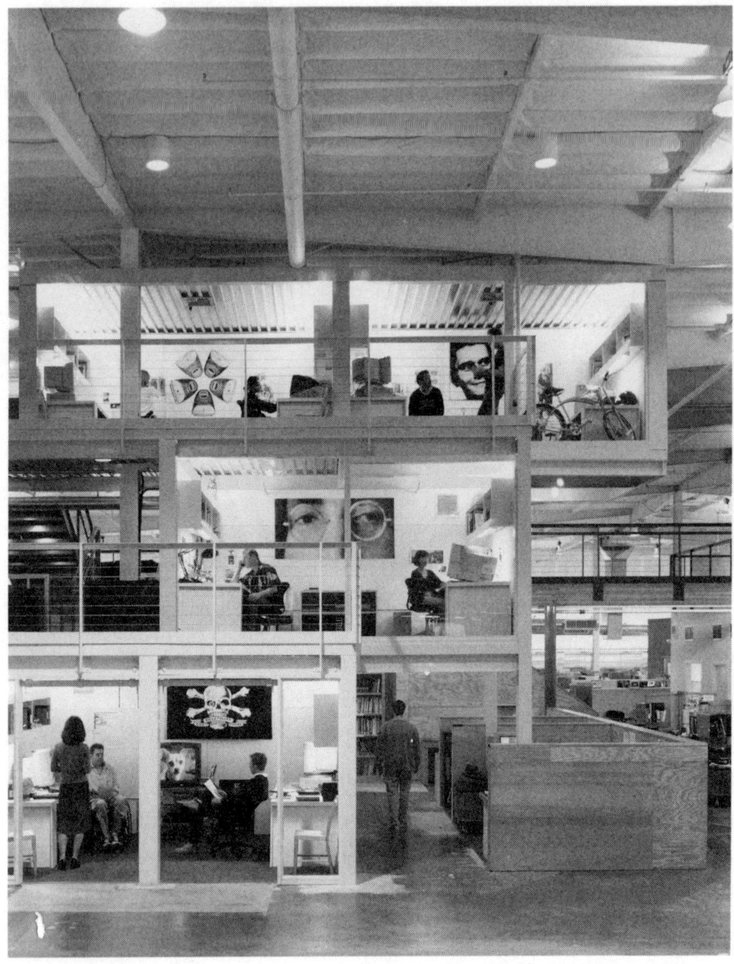

Clive Wilkinson Architects experimented with postmodern metaphors in its office schemes for TBWA Chiat Day (1998), modelled on a 1960s Greenwich Village neighbourhood (above), and Foote, Cone & Belding (2001), a workplace with a waterfront theme (opposite).

the social and the physical within organizations.[6] It is no wonder that Hertzberger was influenced by the anthropologist Claude Lévi-Strauss in conceiving Centraal Beheer. An understanding of how we live was being used to define and design the workplace. When British academics Keith Alexander and Ilfryn Price

later talked about constructing organizational ecologies in the context of facilities management, they were describing a search for community in which the office is a constantly unfolding narrative informed by 'the social practice of use' rather than a fixed technical artefact.[7]

As home to several imaginative community-styled projects designed by Clive Wilkinson and others, California has continued to champion the expensively constructed social democratic office, especially among technology companies operating in Silicon Valley. In 2000, award-winning animation studio Pixar, led by CEO Steve Jobs, relocated to a new studio campus for five hundred people so that all of the film crafts could be united in one large, bright industrial-looking facility with its own 'town square'. Far from separation, people at Pixar were encouraged to meet and bump into each other; serendipity was seen as a benefit and an enabler of new ideas and innovation. Jobs subsequently returned to Apple and began working with architect Sir Norman Foster on a spectacular new headquarters, Apple Park, that would house more than 12,000 employees. This was Jobs's legacy project, a giant circular groundscraper set in a lush natural landscape that opened in Cupertino, California, in April 2017, five years after Jobs's death. Other tech titans, notably Facebook and Google, have also developed expansive new office projects in Silicon Valley, in partnership with leading architects.

Steve Jobs was famously never a fan of remote working. He believed that the best work came from accidentally bumping into other people. 'Creativity comes from spontaneous meetings, from random discussions,' he explained. 'You run into someone; you ask what they're doing, you say "Wow," and soon you're cooking up all sorts of ideas.'[8] That's why he initiated possibly the largest community-orientated office project in the world, one that can be viewed from outer space. Jobs's view on office-based collaboration is echoed by many organizational leaders today who are eager to put remote working, accelerated by the global pandemic, back in its box.

But even as the spectacular Apple Park was coming out of the ground, the classic social democratic model of the office was showing its limitations. Companies facing increasingly volatile business markets began to question such bespoke, inflexible and costly solutions to workspace needs; the community office was fixed in time and place, but the world was moving on. Could a new type of workplace prove a more effective response to the unpredictable patterns of labour generated by knowledge workers using fast-advancing digital technology? So began the third great wave of workplace change, which we describe next as the 'networked office'. After efficiency fever disrupted the genteel world of the nineteenth-century clerk, and constructed social democracy softened the impact of the machine, what would the network do to community?

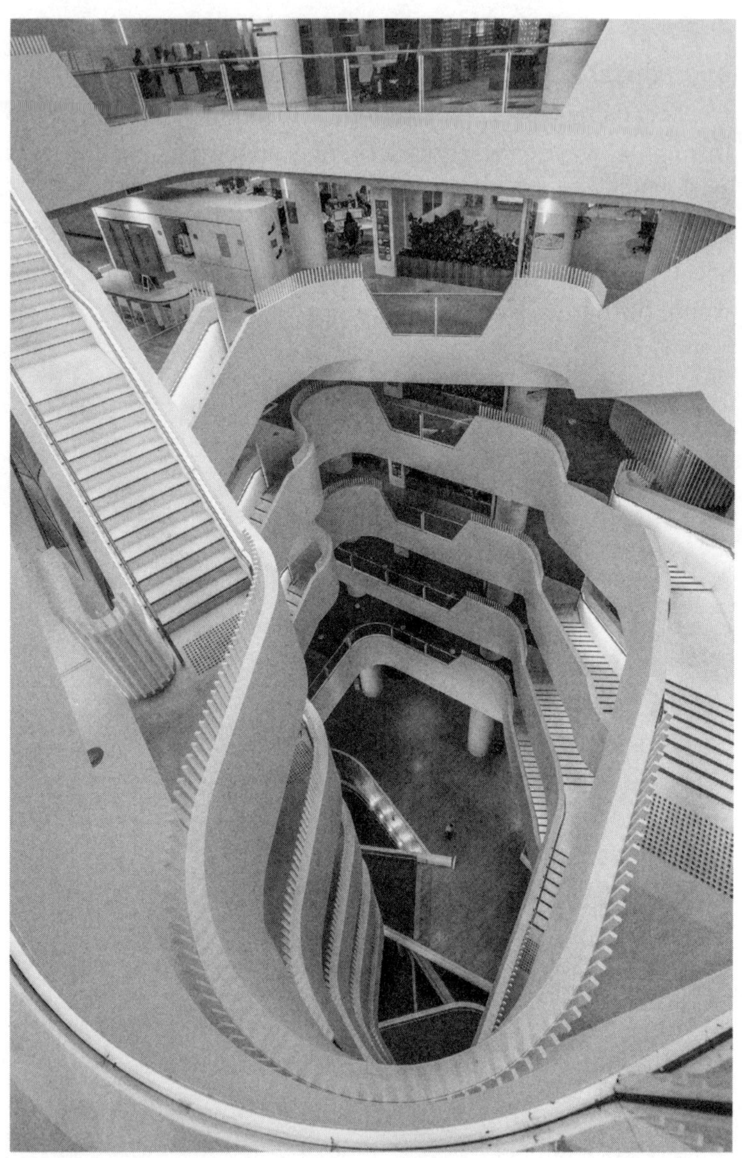

Central atrium of health-insurance provider MediBank's headquarters in Melbourne, designed by Hassell, 2015. It presents the physical embodiment of a social network.

3 Network

By the turn of the new millennium, the modern office, one of the essential artefacts of the twentieth century, was struggling to accommodate fast-changing patterns of work. But there was little consensus among organizations about what to do. Competing workplace strategies jostled for their attention. Companies were worried about reducing office property costs but also concerned about fostering innovation among employees. Employers felt conflicted. Neither paper factories nor faux medieval townscapes nor their various derivatives – all of them based on place, presence and permanence – really met a new workplace challenge with both physical and virtual dimensions. And even though the term 'knowledge work' was already forty years old, having been defined simultaneously but independently by two U.S.-based economists, Peter Drucker and Fritz Machlup, back in 1960, it was widely acknowledged that the workplace didn't really take the specific interactions of knowledge workers seriously enough or fully understand their needs.

It was amid this mixed and contradictory picture that the networked office emerged – and we're living with its essential characteristics today. The networked office repositions the office building as one node in a dynamic organizational network, not a static artefact that stands alone. It is responsive to demand rather than being all about property supply. It is configured to add value to business processes, not to simply accommodate them. Its emphasis is on effectiveness, not just efficiency as in the Taylorist era. It is more flexibly geared to the volatility of business change, with shorter office leases, more flexible space and reconfigurable fittings, than the social democratic model. And for the first time, virtual presence coexists with physical presence in the work environment. Critically, its momentum has been driven neither by developers nor by owner-occupiers, as in previous eras of the office, but by service providers.

The networked office connects an increasingly mobile, tech-enabled workforce with a drop-in place for knowhow and resources, for coaching, mentoring and fostering the collaborations that lead to innovation. In effect, it provides a hub for business and an anchor for corporate culture. It is a place to pass through or to connect to remotely and it is the real manifestation of the organization in an increasingly virtual world. The network has a specific meaning in telecommunications as a system containing a combination of computers and devices to transmit and receive information – and network theory in computing has undoubtedly been an influence on the office. But the implications of the network for the changing office are broader than that. Significantly, it reflects one of the most fundamental shifts of the knowledge economy – the changing nature of work itself, as many people no longer do the kind of repetitive, linear, process-driven work for which the efficiency mantra of scientific management once made perfect sense.

Instead of process work, there is a growing emphasis on knowledge work. This depends less on formula and more on the application of knowledge and learning. Instead of individuals sitting in serried ranks to follow explicit instructions within a supervised hierarchy, new working practices have emerged based on collaboration, initiative and exploration, in which knowledge is often tacit and connections are both inside and beyond the organization. Quickborner's concept of *Bürolandschaft* acknowledged the importance of communication network theory but was bound by the narrow spatial practices and technologies of that era. Later experiments with communities of practice focused on patterns of collaboration and informal social networks within a building or campus without really grasping how knowledge workers operated.

The first people to be identified by Peter Drucker as knowledge workers were doctors, lawyers, academics and scientists. Over the years, large swathes of the managerial and marketing classes would join the knowledge economy. In 2001, Drucker drew attention to a further class of worker he described as 'knowledge technologists': computer technicians, software designers, analysts in clinical labs, paralegals and so on. It is these people who swelled the ranks of knowledge workers worldwide.[1] But at the dawn of a new century, how much did we know about how to design the workspaces for knowledge workers and knowledge-based organizations to be effective? The answer was not very much.

According to a paper in the *MIT Sloan Management Review* in 2002, companies were experimenting heavily with workplace redesign but not learning very much. Co-author Thomas Davenport described most new knowledge work environments as driven by 'fad, fashion and faith'.[2] Drucker himself commented on knowledge-worker productivity: 'We are in the year 2000 roughly where we were in the year 1900 in terms of the productivity of the manual worker.'[3] Given that the productivity of the manual worker increased at least fifty times in the twentieth century, there was a steep climb ahead for the knowledge workplace.

The networked office set out to provide answers to the questions that everyone was asking. It reflected the reality that knowledge workers supported by new digital technologies were breaking free of the traditional fixed office building and working in a new way across a continuum of different locations: corporate campus, public space, home and settings for professional associations and networks. In 2006, we conducted the first global survey of new office design purporting to support knowledge worker performance. We analysed more than forty schemes and identified four 'realms' for knowledge work: the corporate realm (termed 'Academy'), the public realm ('Agora'), the professional realm ('Guild') and the domestic or private realm ('Lodge').[4]

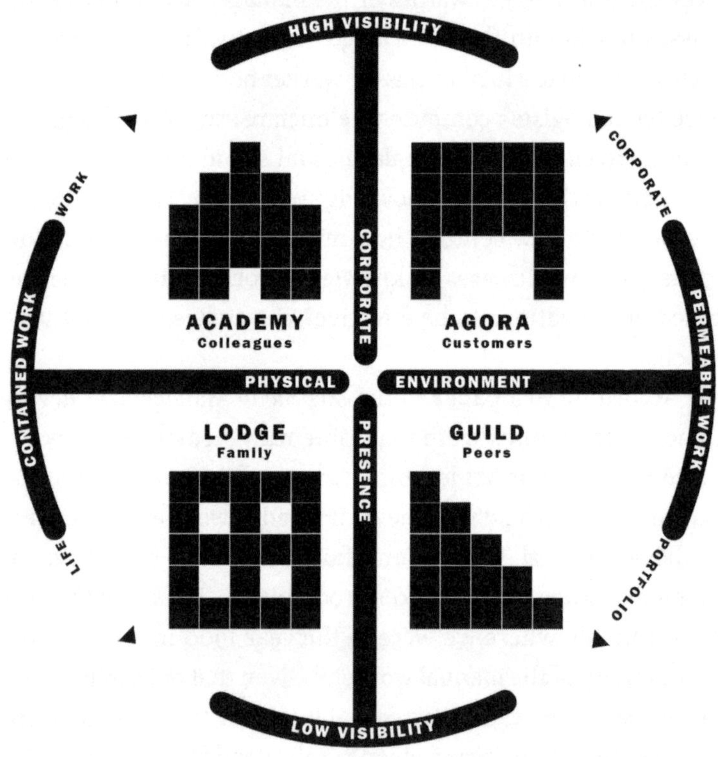

Four realms for knowledge work, from Myerson and Ross, *Space to Work* (2006).

Academy describes a learning campus in which the employer is developing a more collegiate and collaborative approach to work; its historical precedent, in spirit if not in terms of precise architectural template, is the university courtyard or quadrangle. It offers a high level of corporate visibility contained on a specific site, and belongs to the social democratic office tradition. Early adopters included banks, insurance companies, advertising agencies and management consultancies. Agora describes a public workplace in which the company is open to the city and the marketplace; its historical precedent is the commercial and social open space in the heart of ancient Athens. It has a similarly high corporate presence to the Academy but is more permeable in its relationship with its urban context. Early adopters included media, automotive and technology companies.

Guild references a professional cluster of peers who share a skill or specialism; its historical precedent is the medieval guild or craft society, and it combines the characteristics of permeable work with low corporate visibility. Lodge describes the live-work setting, the home that doubles as an office. Its historical precedent is the domestic setting, whether farmhouses or the bourgeois residences that housed the early banks and shipping companies. Lodge is a contained work setting with zero corporate presence. Under-examined compared to the other typologies, it had its time in the spotlight during the COVID-19 pandemic.

We placed all four types of knowledge workplace within a matrix to show how knowledge work could be distributed across an entire network. The ecology of the organization was clearly becoming more complex than ever before. Many different types of organization piloted networked office strategies for more nomadic, self-directed workforces – from the BBC in the UK with its media villages in White City and Salford Quays to the global management consulting firm Accenture. The networked office we know today provides greater flexibility than the social democratic model but perhaps retreats from its levels of individual comfort and group cohesion. It certainly uses new technology to make more efficient, just-in-time use of space than even Frederick Taylor could have imagined. Just as the Taylorist office was centred around the discipline of facilities and space management, and the community office embraced the world of HR, so the networked office came to rely heavily on the IT department.

THE BASIC FOUNDATIONS of the smart or intelligent building, as opposed to a dumb container for work, were established in the early 2000s. The rapid growth of the commercial internet, the proliferation of personal devices such as laptops and mobile phones, an advance in building management systems, and the standardization and roll out of both high-speed cable and wireless networks accounted for the early momentum. In the ten years between 2006 and 2016, a second phase of smart development featured more sophisticated devices like smartphones, and faster connectivity. Technology convergence, open-source software, apps and cloud computing brought the full potential of the networked office into the open.

Today, we're deep into a third phase of the smart building – this is the era of the 'digital ecosystem', and it is being propelled by more powerful and inexpensive computational power than ever before, by billions of connected devices, faster and more widespread connectivity, and huge volumes of data at our fingertips. Smart buildings are commonly described as easier to run, maintain and adapt to change, offering real benefits to occupiers of every type. They give feedback on the occupation and performance of the building in real time, and have some autonomous capacity in using predictive analytics to adjust lighting and heating or reallocate space according to organizational needs. In a sense, these data-driven cornerstones of the networked office, with their location sensors and environmental dashboards, extend the sepia-tinged efficiency story of the 1920s modern office into a new computational realm while simultaneously addressing human needs with a speed and precision that the metaphor-driven designs of the social democratic office could never match.

At the same time as the rise of the smart building put the digital network into the networked office, so the rise of new commercial real-estate practices reconfigured the physical network. Starting in 2005, the year in which the term 'coworking' became recognized as an identifier for shared workspace practices, the workplace sector started experimenting with new models for which the collective term might be 'office as a service'. Although serviced offices had been around for some considerable time, the idea of the office as a service was something new and coworking became its most visible manifestation.

Royal College of Art doctoral researcher Imogen Privett has studied the influence of coworking on office design generally, and she defines coworking as 'the flexible provision of membership-based workplaces where individuals and groups who are not employed by the same organization can share facilities, ideas and knowledge in a communal setting'.[5] Privett's analysis found that the desire to belong to a community was widely and consistently identified as a key factor in the decision to join a coworking space.

Gabor Nagy, while research manager at furniture maker Haworth, analysed the four stages in the evolution of coworking.[6] In the first stage, coworking emerged as a social movement to bring remote workers and freelancers together, out of isolation, and sharing the rent of a larger space. They found that working together and co-ordinating their expertise prompted unexpected innovation. In the second phase, coworking rode the start-up wave as smart entrepreneurs hosted coworking spaces to make a profit – both locally and nationally. Open to the public, these spaces were – and continue to be – membership-based, attracting freelancers, start-ups and some corporate employees. In its third stage, coworking became a mainstream offer: the consumerization of workspace followed when the frontrunners of coworking spaces grew into branded behemoths, such as WeWork and Spaces. In its fourth stage, which we find ourselves in today, the big corporate firms are directly and heavily engaged in coworking: they are not only using flex-space to rethink or reduce their property portfolios amid a rise in remote working caused by the global pandemic, but adopting a coworking-like philosophy in their own workplaces to give their employees a more connected and communal experience.

According to researchers Aurelie Leclercq-Vandelannoitte and Henri Isaac,

> Better than any other previous model of work organisation, coworking spaces address the five conditions that characterise knowledge work: access to information, access to knowledge, access to symbolic resources, access to social capital and opportunities for serendipity . . . they represent a deep change, or even reversal of, the paradigms for work processes in organisations.[7]

As part of a networked office strategy and as a symbol of flexibility, the coworking movement looks set for a bright future after the pandemic.

TO MAKE SENSE of the transitions in office and design culture over the hundred years from the 1920s to the 2020s, it might be worth charting the course of some office typologies. In our work as researchers in the field, we developed our own model of four generic types of organization: the monolith, makeshift, modernizer and mould-breaker.[8] At the end of the twentieth century all four were in evidence. The 'monolith' is a hierarchical organization that is resistant to change, formal and rigid, with private offices for senior managers. It stubbornly clings to the Taylorist model of command and control. The 'makeshift' is a dysfunctional organization in a generally poor standard of accommodation, a Taylorist organization that has basically lost the plot. It is unable to think coherently about redesigning its workspace to meet changing needs and is simply overwhelmed by day-to-day operations. The 'modernizer' could be characterized as a traditional organization (often a monolith) determined to change with the times, usually via relocation to a bright new modern campus or community-based model of working. The 'mould-breaker' is an outlier determined to rewrite the rules of office design by taking a radical new approach to time and place.

Over the past twenty years, the monoliths have been generally in retreat, their inflexible culture and inefficient use of space deemed to be out of touch, especially after the global financial crash of 2008. However, some public-sector and government monoliths survive to this day, as do large private-sector corporations with business monopolies in certain parts of the world, including the USA, South Korea and Japan. Makeshift organizations unable to reform, meanwhile, have been largely blown away by the global competitive pressures and pace of change. This has been the era, then, of the modernizers and, to a lesser extent, the mould-breakers.

A number of powerful trends related to modernization, chiefly around ideas of social interaction, exchange, collaborative buzz and community, have been vigorously promoted through new schemes. The modernizers, increasingly locked in a global race for talent, have also paid closer attention to employee health and well-being. Mental health in particular has shot up the agenda in British and American workplaces. Biophilic design, an idea that has been around since the 1980s to bring workers closer to nature in all its forms, has made a big comeback – workplace designers have introduced plants and trees into the interior environment, improved natural ventilation and access to natural light, and specified natural materials and imagery (see p. 142). In 2018, Amazon went further than anyone else by creating The Spheres, three interconnected spherical conservatories, as part of its urban Seattle HQ. Designed by architects NBBJ and filled with 40,000 plants, this 'cloud forest' is a place for Amazon employees to wander, wonder and be inspired – a natural workplace that fills the senses and provides a conducive place to connect with colleagues or do focused work. The Spheres adjoin an Amazon campus building called Day 1, a reference to the year-zero concept of unworking we introduced at the start of this book.

Some genuine mould-breakers gradually emerged in the period up to the 2020s. These companies, clustered in the media and tech industries, were few in number and primarily interested in creating experiences rather than just providing space; they went beyond modernization to ask fundamental questions about the purpose of the office. Their 'sweetspot' was a combination of health-inducing physical design features and sensor technologies capable of tracking occupancy and adapting environmental conditions. They lessened reliance on standard corporate office space, mixing up their real-estate portfolios with coworking memberships and short, flex-space leases as part of the office-as-a-service model. They invested in digital transformation, portable devices and video-first technologies, and the training to go with that investment. So, of course, they were in the best position to withstand the shock of the coronavirus pandemic that brought economies around the world to a standstill overnight and sent workforces scurrying to work from home during lockdown.

What, then, of the future? Where does the modern office go next on its journey of reinvention? Makeshift firms have largely gone to the wall and it is clear that we shouldn't look to the monoliths or the modernizers for clues. If companies cannot modernize, they will become obsolete. Equally, if they are still trying to modernize, it could already be too late. The answers lie with the mould-breakers.

PART II

WHAT COMES NEXT

Burning Man, an awe-inspiring collaborative effort in Nevada's Black Rock Desert from which large employers have tried to learn how to create a memorable collaborative experience.

4 Experience

In all the debates about the evolution of office design over the course of a century, one thing that barely rated consideration was the experience of the people working in these spaces. Scientific management was in no doubt who was in control in an often brutal economic exchange, and even the social democratic impulses which later softened the edges of the workplace did not fundamentally change the nature of the social contract between companies and their employees. The old joke about nobody on their deathbed ever wishing they'd spent more time in the office may be well worn, but it has more than an element of truth. We've spent time in the office out of economic necessity, not because we've enjoyed it. Indeed, one of the side effects of efficiency theory was to make the work aesthetic reflect the work ethic – stern, unbending, monotonous, focused only on overcoming frustration and staying on the task.

But what if we could make the office experience in the future more pleasurable, more engaging, more fun even? In Joseph Heller's famous 1974 novel *Something Happened*, which presents the interior monologue of a troubled businessman preparing for a promotion at work, the main character observes, 'It's a real problem to decide whether it's more boring to do something boring than to pass along everything boring that comes in to somebody else and then have nothing to do at all.'[1] Heller sums up a quintessential feature of the workplace as routine, dull and repetitive, one in which new experiences rarely come along.

Indeed, in the many decades after Heller's novel was published, offices barely improved in the quality of experience. People by and large continued to do the same things, at the same time, in the same place, by the same route, day after working day – at least until the global coronavirus pandemic gave cause to rethink. Basic functional considerations such as furnishing, ergonomics, spatial layout, lighting and technology might have been upgraded, but little specific attention was given to the wider experiential dimension of the workplace and its impact on behaviour, motivation and performance.

Today, however, the subject of workplace experience is rising fast up the business agenda. From a very low base – user experience simply wasn't on the map in most organizations a few years ago – there is now a burgeoning industry focused on it. There are even new job titles emerging inside organizations, such as the CXO ('chief experience officer') or 'vibe manager'. The American designer Kelly Robinson, who was vibe manager at the Berlin office of SoundCloud, an online audio platform, told us why experience has become more important for employers: 'The exterior environment affects the inner self.' According to Robinson, we can expect offices to provide more things like yoga, mindfulness, cry rooms, music rooms and spaces to grow your own food – all of which needs curating by people in new job roles.[2]

When British Airways opened its Waterside office, the airline announced the appointment of a corporate jester, to general bafflement. However, it was an early example of a new job title which hinted that the experience of work could be fun. Management consultant David Firth, co-author of *The Corporate Fool*

(1998), told us that there is a place in organizational life for the contrarian or satirist who is a confidante of the leader but will do the undoable, think the unthinkable and say the unsayable. This points to a more human, fallible side of work.

Confronted with corporate jokers and vibe curators as clients, the developers, designers and managers of workspaces are now entering unfamiliar territory – no longer simply part of the global facilities industry but part of an 'experience economy'. New roles are emerging on the supply side, too: Adam Scott is an 'experience masterplanner' with FreeState, part of the Hassell architectural firm. He told us: 'People want live, stimulating, engaging and meaningful experiences because these elements create a sense of belonging.' For property professionals who have long prided themselves on applying hard metrics to the built infrastructure, the idea that they should behave like a branch of the entertainment or hospitality business in providing 'experiences' for employees can be difficult to get their heads around. But we believe this is where offices are heading.

THERE ARE SPECIFIC reasons why organizations should think about providing better workplace experiences. In a digital economy with a premium on top talent, where every company is essentially a digital company (even a bank or a legal practice), firms are competing to attract the best people with an experiential offer that includes free food, curated events and 'cool' office interiors. There is growing imperative to innovate – and a recognition that the familiar day-to-day experiences of even well-planned offices and campuses are not conducive to encouraging people to think differently or seek different colleagues and partners to generate new ideas. So new experiences are being designed that support innovation, such as the provision of project rooms, creative labs and spaces for chance encounters.

Organizations trying to maintain employee performance and morale amid the economic chaos wrought by the global pandemic are increasingly focused on health and well-being to improve productivity. Workplace experience is critical in this context, so we're seeing more biophilic environments, cleaner air, daylighting, soundscapes, stress helplines, health checks, retreat spaces for mindfulness and yoga or Pilates classes, as Kelly Robinson predicted. In an unstable era of rapid change, workforces constantly need to update their knowledge both online and in group-learning settings. So companies are also looking at learning experiences, with a focus on lifelong learning and self-learning in the workplace. Experiences for learning include immersive learning suites and social learning events.

One effect of the pandemic has been to accelerate the use of automation and artificial intelligence in the office, which in theory leaves people to concentrate on more imaginative and creative types of work. This type of work will necessarily be more social and collaborative, making the office a 'destination' of choice for employees who have the option to access their data from the cloud and work remotely from anywhere.

Whatever the business reasons, many different new experiences are set to emerge in the workplace. Just as online shopping has disrupted the physical retail experience, so digital disruption in the workplace has begun to affect office design. Indeed, many of the customer-centric techniques of retail and hospitality – with an emphasis on responding swiftly to real-time data – are transferring to the office. Companies that once focused only on the experience and service their customers in the market received are now rethinking what they give to their employees in the workplace.

When we studied this phenomenon closely in a research project with Australian property company Mirvac,[3] we saw organizations in many sectors upping their game on experience.

Before the shock of the COVID-19 crisis in 2020, the main reason cited by company leaders was the race for talent; after, it was the need to bring people back to the office in a safe and effective manner after prolonged periods of working from home and to make the office a competitive and compelling alternative to remote working.

We coined the term 'super-experience' to describe a shift from UX (User Experience) to SX (Super Experience); and we defined the super-experience as a workplace experience of superior quality, originality and impact, appealing on an emotional level as well as an intellectual one. Often super-experiences combine physical and digital elements. They can make you feel excited or that you've achieved something; they can stimulate curiosity, create a sense of purpose or instil a sense of belonging. They can be incongruous and unexpected, or reassuring in terms of people's expectations. They can be small and intimate or executed on a grand scale.

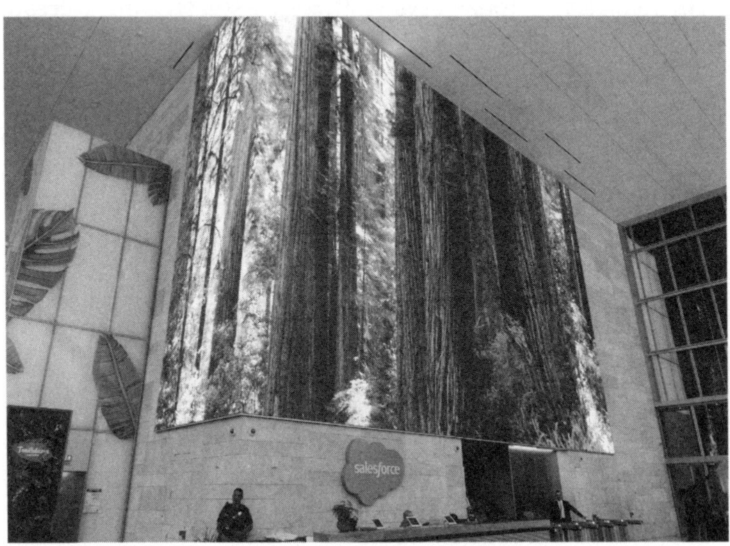

Spectacular immersive video of redwood forests in the lobby of Salesforce's San Francisco office: super-experiences are on the rise.

Step into the lobby of Salesforce's San Francisco office, for example, and you're confronted with a giant digital wall that can display a Redwood National Park forest scene in high resolution or mimic a convincing waterfall. Ride the elevator at One World Trade Center in New York and, as you climb 102 floors in 47 seconds, you're immersed in an astonishing audio-visual experience as you witness the urban growth and development of the city from the 1500s to the present day. Look up in Bloomberg's London office and the ceiling comprises 2.5 million polished aluminium 'petals' to regulate acoustics, temperature and light. These are all what we might term 'super-experiences' in the workplace.

Adam Scott of FreeState believes that 'the first great super-designed experience took place 30,000 years ago in caves lit by fire and overseen by Shamans. The Shaman was a master of designed experiences – fierce, awesome and ecstatic experiences which bound people together and to something greater than themselves.' Today, says Scott, we are still striving to create the 'unforgettable moment' that invites the spectator into the spectacle. Architect Ali Ganjavian of Studio Banana, whose firm created the Momentum Experience Centre in EY's London headquarters, told us that 'super-experiences in the workplace are those that allow people to try something new for the first time and shift their behaviour and way of thinking as a result'.

Historically, the experience of the modern office was all about combining clarity with optimization. The principle was to make processes and facilities easy and clear to understand and use, while optimizing resources. This served organizational efficiency very well. Today, however, we would argue that experiences should sit along a spectrum. Experiences should have levels of intrigue, delight and curiosity – not just clarity, which can be dull and routine. Experiences should be empathic in terms of sensing and responding to other people's emotions, and not just all about optimizing resources.

Super-experiences are therefore emerging as workplace experience focuses less on the traditional values of clarity and optimisation and more on intrigue and empathy. Experiences that combine greater empathy with some element of intrigue or curiosity can be seen in particular to support organizational innovation, as individual creativity and imagination is unleashed in partnership with trust and empowerment. It explains why spaces for innovation sometimes look more relaxed, friendly and informal than a normal office space, as softer seating, lower

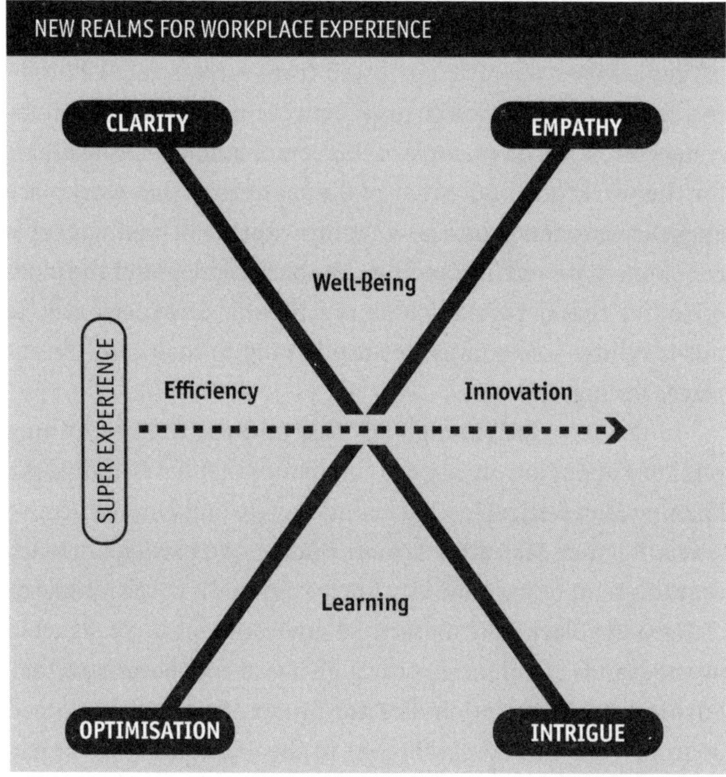

Super-experiences aim beyond efficiency. Diagram published by Worktech Academy/Mirvac (2020).

light levels, adaptable furniture or fittings and artworks and artefacts about the place stimulate and inspire.

Super-experiences can support other company needs. A combination of clarity and empathy, for example, can be seen to create a strong foundation for well-being, as empathic spaces such as rest areas and services for better health are given clear visual priority in the workplace. A combination of optimization and intrigue can lead to new learning experiences – a state-of-the-art corporate learning space with immersive audio-visual technology, for example, that can stimulate the appetite for knowledge in large numbers of people at the same time.

Let's not forget that the intersection of clarity and optimization still holds plenty of relevance in the workplace: the provision of 'genius bars' – a term borrowed from Apple's retail stores – inside offices, where you go to get your technology fixed and stay connected, is a good example of this combination being desirable for the workforce. But what really matters is that workplace experience extends into new realms capable of taking people out of one state and into another. The back catalogue of the modern office does not yield rich source material on experience – to put it mildly – so companies are having to look in different places for inspiration.

In the USA, for example, Google and the online clothing retailer Zappos are among the companies that have studied the Burning Man festival in a bid to find ways to build more effective teams. Burning Man attracts more than 50,000 participants each year to a temporary mini-city for the arts built in the middle of of Nevada's Black Rock Desert. Its environment is constructed by thousands of volunteers through a vast collaborative effort. Burning Man's education director Stuart Mangrum explained in 2018: 'Behavioural psychology in the workplace has largely been Pavlovian and Taylorist – to get people to do what you want them to do. Burning Man is about intrinsic motivation and radical inclusion. The downside is that we are inefficient, but we are intentionally inefficient. We are building a lasting culture.'[4]

The experience of Burning Man can be described as awe-inspiring. An important dimension of the super-experience is the ability to create a sense of awe. We're accustomed to using the adjective 'awesome' to describe cathedrals, museums, opera houses or upscale homes, but rarely employ it when discussing workplaces. This is likely to change as more organizations understand the benefits that a sense of awe can bring to the workplace.

Researchers Vladas Griskevicius, Michelle Shiota and Samantha Neufeld define a sense of awe as 'the feeling of wonder and astonishment experienced in the presence of something novel and difficult to grasp – a stimulus that cannot be accounted for by one's current understanding of the world.'[5] According to different academic studies, employees think more creatively, are more curious and process information more efficiently when they are confronted by objects or spaces that inspire a sense of awe.[6] People also have a more open mind, are less impatient, feel more connected to the world around them, integrate more effectively into social groups, have a more balanced view of their strengths and weaknesses and experience greater momentary well-being.

This growing body of scientific evidence to support the idea that a sense of awe in the workplace can boost employee performance is significant because it introduces an economic rationale for design features that are not just out of the ordinary but sometimes out of this world. Design proposals for a genuinely jaw-dropping feature or setting have often been dismissed as self-indulgent, which is why some of the most spectacular elements of new workplace schemes tend to be engineered out of the process at an early stage on the grounds of cost. But now the mood is changing, and some spectacular innovations in the workplace are seeing the light of day.

The trouble with being awestruck, however, is that there could be diminishing returns in the workplace as employees repeat the same experiences day after day. The first time you view something that takes your breath away is when you really experience that sense of awe. It doesn't happen often but you know the feeling when you get it. The next time, it becomes marginally less astonishing. By the fiftieth time, it's probably become the new normal.

However, creating a sense of awe doesn't depend on scale; academic research suggests that even the smallest things – an intricately crafted jewellery box, for example – can produce the same sensation. Nor does it depend on quickening the emotions. Giving employees an oasis in which to slow down, pause and reflect during the working day can also be awe-inspiring. Conducting user research among employees to determine the potential effects of any intervention is important. Experiences that successfully encourage people to behave in new ways by shaking up their psychology are often a result of co-design or consultation processes with those employees. NASA, for example, set up the International Space Orchestra under the direction of experience designer Nelly Ben Hayoun to coax its scientists out of their usual thinking patterns through music and performance.

EXPERIENCES USED TO JUST happen in the workplace, without much planning or control, almost as a by-product of what went on throughout the day. Today, influenced in part by COVID-19 pandemic, experiences are set to become highly curated and stage-managed, often enabled by an app and delivered by specialist providers. Some of that precision and sophistication reflects the rising influence of the global coworking movement, which has grown rapidly by providing experience-driven workspaces for people who work outside traditional corporate structures. Coworking can be viewed as critique of workplaces that have traditionally placed a lower priority on such issues as service, community and purpose. Coworking venues live or die by what their customers think of the experience – if members are unimpressed, they can simply take their trade elsewhere.

Just consider what a start-up company gets by joining a coworking venue: a shorter, more flexible lease; a designed environment that it does not have to fit out itself; and access to people and resources (including venture capital injected by the coworking provider in some cases) that will be useful to help their business grow. Many coworking members belong to a gig economy in which they have several jobs in a range of places and can choose the experience that fits the task they are currently working on. Compare the fast and informal service typically offered by community managers at WeWork or one of its competitors with the grumpy janitorial approach to facilities management found inside many corporate organizations: it is little surprise that many corporate employees today opt to work at least partially in coworking spaces, and that many corporate organizations are seeking to create a cowork-style vibe within their own office buildings.

While much coworking-inspired workplace curation borrows from the hospitality sector, many ideas are also being imported from retail. The mapping of customer journeys and the suggestions of new experiences (things to do and people to meet) via digital apps transfer the customer focus of retail into the heart of the workplace. Much like how IKEA stores curate a route for customers to move throughout the store, the tech giants have started to adopt a similar concept to curate their employees' workplace experience. Mapping journeys throughout the building can help create a better, more human workplace experience.

Other companies are emulating Netflix, which recommends programmes for individuals based on what they have previously watched or what others have enjoyed by developing workplace apps to create 'suggested experiences'. This is where employees are presented with a range of options on their smartphones on where to work and whom to meet in the office, based on what they have previously done, their job function and what they need to do. A series of recommendations are given based on algorithms from machine-learning software, all designed to make the workplace experience more enjoyable and purposeful. Sodexo, for example, the French food services and facilities giant, has introduced a workplace app for employee devices in its Stockholm and Oslo offices that proactively helps in various ways at work, such as nudging people towards interactions with colleagues or highlighting food options near their location. In the age of experience, algorithms will increasingly predict, suggest, prompt and nudge our every move based on past behaviour and recorded preferences.

ULTIMATELY, THE FUTURE of workplace experience will require not just a new outlook by those who develop and lease out office buildings, but a culture change at the top of the major companies that occupy them. According to a global survey by Deloitte of business leaders across 140 countries, more company executives accept that employee experience is very important than believe that their own organization is doing a decent job at getting it right.[7] There is much ground to make up and many things will need to change. The office property sector was caught off guard by the rising focus on experience, and we predict that it will need to widen its skill base by bringing in new expertise and ideas from theatre, arts, hospitality, retail and behavioural science. There will also need to be a more open mind regarding what technologies to adopt, as the search for super-experiences will require new lighting, AV, soundscaping and sensor technologies to be introduced to the workplace along with a profusion of digital apps.

Inside companies, there will need to be a shake-up of the traditional departments of FM (facilities management), IT (information technology) and HR (human resources), which have operated in silos and either ignored or competed with each other for too long. Providing a great workplace experience depends on a mesh of space, technology and people policies. These disciplines are all integral to experience and need to work together in a much more concerted way. Or, as many experts propose, they should be disbanded and consolidated into one unified workplace management or, better still, workplace experience service. Whatever route organizations decide to take, improving the experience of work will be one of the primary levers of change in the future office.

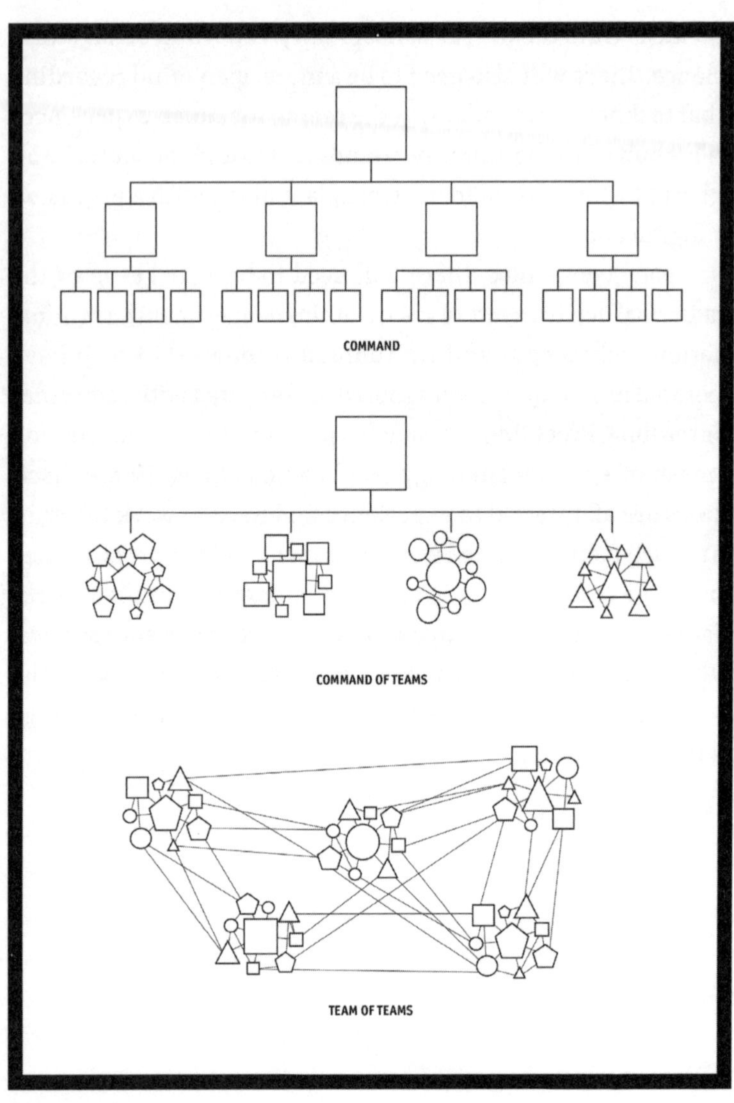

Moving from a hierarchy to agile teams, from Stanley McChrystal, *Team of Teams* (2015).

5 Organization

Organizations themselves are not immune to reinvention. In the era of the modern office, they have sought to present themselves as the epitome of permanence, solidity and longevity. Even though the majority of employment in most economies is within the so-called SME (small and medium-sized enterprises) sector, big business and multinational corporations have dominated the concept of work and defined the essence of employment. It is in this realm where benevolent paternalism has historically been an expectation for those seeking a career – the classic salaryman in Japanese society or 'wage slave' in Western economies expected to be looked after as the trade-off for providing human capital. School leavers or university graduates were employed as apprentices or trainees and many worked their way up the corporate ladder with the expectation of a 'job for life'.

As part of collective responsibility, employers provided benefits from pensions to health care; as the Industrial Revolution spawned vast conglomerates, many companies constructed homes and schools for their employees, with the Lever Brothers' Port Sunlight (1888) and Cadbury's Bournville (1895) both famous examples from Britain's industrial past. These systems, where work-life blurred in the pursuit of utopia and commerce, created vast bureaucratic systems to manage the organization.

For some, this is coming full circle, with the Silicon Valley tech giants once again creating campuses where people can work, socialize, learn, eat and, soon, live or sleep. Facebook, for example, is building a new village campus at Menlo Park with 1,700 homes. A variant on the conservatism of the industrial pioneers that often had its roots in religion or profession, employer benevolence first developed as both blue- and white-collar work expanded, and skills previously performed by individuals were clustered together for the collective benefits of efficiency and performance.

The Quakers were early purveyors of paternalism. Rowntree's became one of the biggest confectioners in the world and was a pioneer of worker well-being. Like Cadbury (another Quaker organization), they provided welfare for their workers ranging from dentists to entertainment, social events and outings. Education was integral to the approach, with libraries and schools

The Port Sunlight model village on the Wirral Peninsula on Merseyside, built by Lever Brothers from 1888 onwards. The edges of working and living were blurred as part of a paternalistic approach.

built for employees, and the strategy eventually included housing for workers with the creation of Rowntree's famous model village, New Earswick. Quakerism shaped many modern businesses, from Barclays Bank to Friends Provident, and instilled a rigour for management that was defined by their puritanism and philanthropy.

As complex organizations emerged, whether commercial, military or in health care, complex structures developed to allow effective management. A corporate hierarchy illustrated by the organizational chart mapped out the corporation and its strata, departments and reporting lines. This formality created the modern workplace as a study in structure and solidity. Typically, if you projected an organizational structure diagram (known as the 'org chart') onto the side of a building, it would show how the space was organized: an executive floor at the top, followed by layers of the organization based by department and, at the base, the meeting rooms that bring everyone together.

Stratification was a common thread in hierarchy, and with each additional rung came status and privilege. Tiers of management created a 'them and us' mentality, reinforced by physical demarcations of seniority – the trappings of success. These were often represented by the workplace, where space and status became intertwined. Command and control was the mantra of management. Today, however, this organizational rule book is being ripped up. Companies are learning about more fluid management structures from people like General Stanley McChrystal, who told us about his experience leading the U.S. armed forces in Afghanistan and Iraq.[1]

During the hunt for al-Qaeda in Iraq, McChrystal realized that the formality of the military command-and-control structure was too cumbersome and too slow to make decisions against an agile enemy. So he reordered his command to form fluid self-empowered teams that made decisions and got results. In his book *Team of Teams*, McChrystal reflects that 'when we established our Task Force headquarters at Balad, we hung maps on almost every wall. Maps are sacred to a soldier.' But they realized that these maps didn't depict the battlefield of a terrorist organization. 'In place of maps, whiteboards began to appear . . . we thought out loud diagramming what we knew. In place of the straight lines and right angles of a military command, we found ourselves drawing tangled networks that did not resemble any organisational structures we had ever seen.'

At his central command centre at Balad in Iraq, McChrystal created one big workspace so everyone could come together, optimizing the flow of information and speed of decision making.

> Balad was a beautiful opportunity: a place to build something entirely new, the physical manifestation of the organisational system that might tilt the odds in our favour. As we sat in our makeshift command centre in Balad . . . we realised that our goal was not the creation of one massive team. We needed to create a *team of teams*.[2]

Frederick Taylor had bequeathed the org chart to the military as well as the corporation – here was a decisive break with the past. McChrystal was a leader who recognized that, by the time a decision had passed up through the traditional chain of command, the enemy had vanished. So instead of the layers of hierarchy, he created fluid, autonomous, connected teams that could react swiftly on the ground and used a makeshift workspace to orchestrate the flow. McChrystal now advises large businesses on how to disrupt command-and-control management structures.

LEADERSHIP IS OFTEN CONSTRAINED within the organization, isolated through spatial barriers and protected by layers of 'middle management' that provide the filters and only report upwards, not down. The pyramid representing this hierarchy also typically reflects the separation that is designed into the organizational environment. Creating separation, remoteness and celebrating status was the emphasis, from the 'corner office' with deeper-piled carpet to the private dining room, the executive toilet or washroom and reserved car parking space. Corporate offices became representations of power and prowess.

When Sony launched the Walkman in 1979, its success was astonishing. Achieving sales of over 20 million units in the first few heady years, Sony's leaders Akio Morita and Masaru Ibuka had taken a risk with their invention and it had paid off. Working from the basement of a department store in Tokyo, they believed in boundary-free brainstorming with the engineers that produced the technology. But Sony's success created a conglomerate with more than 160,000 people, eventually producing a plethora of innovations including the Trinitron television, Vaio computer and PlayStation alongside the Walkman. It was split into divisions based on these winning products – all, essentially, stand-alone organizations.

A consequence of this approach was that collaboration halted. With management responsible for their own profit-and-loss accounts, they set out to protect their own units within the Sony corporation. In Gillian Tett's book *The Silo Effect*, she reflects that, although Sony used the slogan 'Sony United', 'different departments became less and less willing to interact. This in turn made the boundaries of the silos more rigid. Outside the walls of the electronics giant, the world of entertainment, media and electronics was changing fast . . . but inside the company, the departmental walls were hardening.'[3]

When Sony co-founder Masaru Ibuka set up the original business that would become Sony in 1958, his prospectus said that the 'purpose of incorporation was to create an ideal workplace that was free, dynamic and joyous'. Fifty years later, the sheer size and success of Sony led to entrenched boundaries. As the internet reshaped entertainment technology, each division worked on its own innovations. Sony Music (created from the acquisition of CBS Records) didn't talk to the Walkman division who didn't talk to the Vaio division. At a time when it was widely recognized that entrenched silos could damage not just innovation but the essence and spirit of the organization, Sony's divisions stayed separate.

The situation at Sony could not have been more different to that at Apple, fast becoming a global industrial competitor with founder Steve Jobs back at the helm. As Walter Isaacson observes in his book on Jobs, 'The phrases [Jobs] used were "deep collaboration" and "concurrent engineering." Instead of a development process in which a product would be passed sequentially from engineering to design to manufacturing to marketing and distribution, these various departments collaborated simultaneously.'[4] Jobs's legacy project for Apple, the shiny new campus headquarters in Cupertino, California, was designed as a circular workplace where continuous collaboration is at the heart of the work process.

When, in 2001, Apple launched the iPod, it sealed the fate of Sony's leadership. A British CEO was appointed soon afterwards. As Tett describes, in Sir Howard Stringer's first speech, he described Sony as a 'company with too many silos'. Introspection and internal division had allowed the great pioneer to be overtaken by both Apple and Samsung. Sony had both the music catalogue and the technology to do what Apple did with iTunes, but the management structures got in the way.

The poet Lao Tzu is said to have remarked: 'In the highest antiquity, the people did not know that there were rulers. In the next age they loved them and praised them. In the next they feared them; in the next they despised them.' The secret of successful organizations is to maintain the first phases and not allow it all to go downhill. Organizations need leaders and entrepreneurs to take risks, generate growth, set the corporate vision and provide direction. But they may not need the rigid structures and hierarchy to maintain the new direction.

At the Las Vegas-based online shoe and clothing retailer Zappos, founder and former CEO Tony Hsieh created a new organizational model based on the concept of holacracy, a method of decentralized management and organizational governance with no hierarchy, no managers and no job titles. Decision making was distributed through the organization, aimed at providing both resilience and 'hyper-productivity'. Now owned by Amazon, the Zappos model has evolved, but it still creates an approach that is based on independent teams rather than centralized bureaucracy. People work in tribes and manage their own money, and so act as small entrepreneurial businesses, even if they are part of a big machine. In this way, they are empowered to drive customer-centric thinking that is essential to the Zappos business. The company, in effect, created an internal market where groups trade with each other.

Hsieh's vision extended into physical space with his Downtown Project in Las Vegas – he took over the old City Hall for Zappos' new headquarters in a run-down neighbourhood north of the Strip. Here he invested more than U.S.$350 million of his own money to revitalize and reimagine the urban realm to make Downtown Vegas a place of 'inspiration, creativity and entrepreneurial energy'. At the centre of the scheme is the Container Park, an outdoor shopping complex built from repurposed shipping containers that now sit underneath a giant sculptural fire-breathing praying mantis – a design inspired by the Burning Man festival. Container Park houses around thirty small businesses and start-ups.

Hsieh talked about a 'return on collisions' with the value of unplanned encounters quantified in a way that echoes the vision at Boston Consulting Group's Hudson Yards workspace in New York, where a 'collision coefficient' was established as a scientific method to measure the number and effect of random encounters in the company. The Downtown Project encouraged innovation that was driven by the fabric of the spaces Hsieh funded – in effect the city as start-up. Alongside the Container Park, a former casino called the Gold Spike was turned into a coworking hub and a festival – Life Is Beautiful – was set up. The project resonated with a creative energy that was evident in Hsieh's book, *Delivering Happiness: A Path to Profits, Passion and Purpose* (2010), which talks of the need to make customer service the responsibility of the entire organization and not just one department.

A similar approach was adopted by Chinese manufacturing giant Haier. The firm recognized that size is no protection against failure and wanted to instil in its employees an ability to achieve self-realization. As Zhang Ruimin, the founding CEO of Haier, asked: 'Do people just passively come to work every day as requested? Or do they actively come here to fulfil their ambitions? Part of making sure it's the latter is having the right organizational structure – one that is as boundaryless and flat as possible.'[5] And so the company formed project teams that were focused on the market – people answered to the customer and not their superior. 'That is not an easy orientation to bring about,' Zhang reflected.

Haier employees are paid bonuses based on the results of their teams rather than the usual position-based compensation system. Zhang's vision is that 'the enterprise will become great when it is able to operate by itself, with employees acting as their own leaders, understanding what to do to satisfy market and customer demand.' Indeed, self-organization and self-adaptive systems are a growing trend as work tasks become more complex and difficult to standardize – and managers expect employees to deal with them independently and self-sufficiently.

IN HIS 1896 ARTICLE 'The Tall Office Building Artistically Considered', the American architect Louis Sullivan, one of the fathers of Modernism, used the axiom 'form follows function' and talked of the idea that architecture should accommodate discrete cells in the organizational structure.[6] Although climbing the corporate ladder was once synonymous with success, other models with flatter organizational structures, self-empowered teams and the practice of holacracy now provide alternative perspectives. What form of workplace should follow the way these new organizational structures work?

McKinsey & Co. states, in its article 'The Journey to an Agile Organization', that 'traditional organizations are built around a static, siloed, structural hierarchy, whereas agile organizations are characterized as a network of teams operating in rapid learning and decision-making cycles.'[7] McKinsey goes on to recognize that 'an agile organization doesn't deliver work according to a classic organization chart; rather, it can be thought of as a series of cells grouped around common milestones, often called "tribes".'

Self-contained teams using an agile approach have been a feature of software development for some time. Agile scrum methodology sees quick software releases resulting from sprints in a 'fail fast' mentality that speeds up time to market. Small agile teams working in specific agile spaces are beginning to redefine the workplace for team endeavour. As McKinsey recognizes, 'Agile team members will likely need to co-locate and will require a workspace to enable agile ways of working and collaboration with other cells.'

Most organizations mask teamwork with meetings. When you sit day-by-day in the office with your departmental colleagues, but work on multidisciplinary projects, you spend your life going to meetings, usually held in soulless rooms that bear no reference to the project but provide a vehicle for reporting and minute-taking in a formulaic approach that hasn't changed for the best part of a century. Contrast this to a scenario where the project team sits together for the duration. Immediate decisions, better communication through overheard conversations, and the swift sharing of ideas and data produce better results faster and with fewer risks. But most workplaces have not provided these agile project environments – just endless ranks of desks and corridors of meeting rooms. What if we could plan workplaces based on the interactions and ideas of the communities and tribes that form the organization in motion?

Charles Handy has written widely about organizations and the future of the firm. In his book *The Empty Raincoat*, first published in 1994, Handy predicts the rise of the gig economy, shows us the 'shamrock' organization and demonstrates a future organizational structure based on a stable core and more flexible periphery, that is, a business split across different groups: a continuous, set group of managers and technicians who hold detailed knowledge of the organization, a group of contracted workers and, furthest out from the centre, a group of more casual employees.

In his follow-up *Gods of Management* (1996), Handy discusses different organizational cultures, reflecting on the tension between more formal bureaucracies and more entrepreneurial cultures driven by the charisma of the founder. Handy illustrates these differences using the Greek gods: Apollo, to reflect wisdom in a culture where people crave stability and certainty; Zeus, the supreme god, which represents the classic founder culture; Dionysus, the god of dance, pleasure and wine, to symbolize the professions where skilled, experienced people often have independence; and finally Athena, also wise but notably the goddess of peace, for a collegiate, problem-solving culture.

Athena is perhaps where the future of the workplace aligns most closely: this is a view of the organization as a collection of tasks or activities, performed in configured spaces within an organizational network that resembles ever-changing clusters – the teams that form and disband to get work done. It is a fluid interpretation that borrows from tribes of ancient history. Co-operation and collaboration are fundamental. People come together to perform discrete tasks. Expertise and experience trump status and role in a results- or output-based culture achieved through team endeavour.

These communities of purpose will increasingly use AI tools to automate or augment work tasks and processes. The organization will be shaped by analytics and machine intelligence that will predict the optimal way in which work should be done. Self-forming and forever in flux, the workplace must accommodate

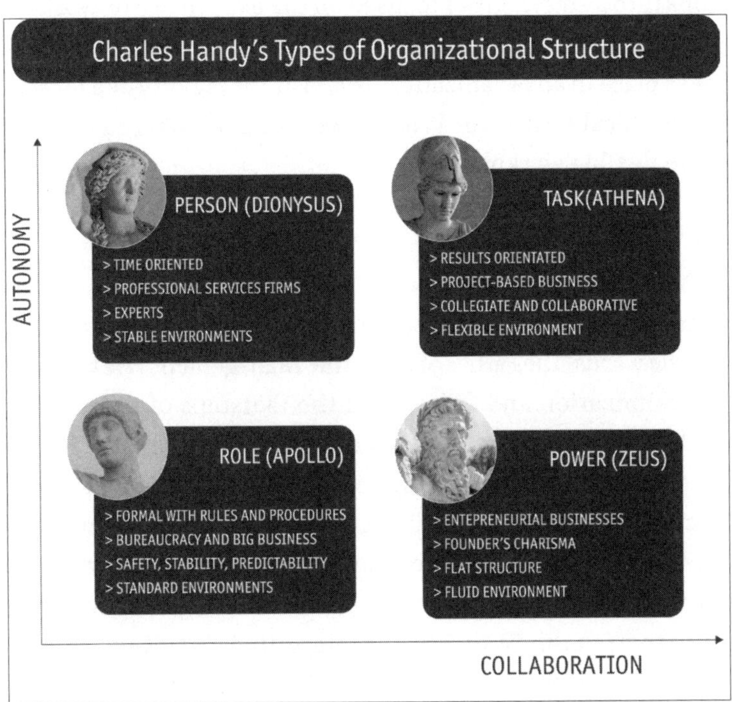

Greek gods illustrate four different types of organizational culture, from Charles Handy, *Gods of Management* (1996).

uncertainty rather than the more formulaic and predictable structures evident in Charles Handy's taxonomy.

There is room for all the gods in the workplace, but their role will increasingly be determined by a new model of clustering based on the real work undertaken and not the static organizational chart. A building needs to accommodate an elastic workforce, and so needs to be adaptable. The structures that created the silos are a part of the problem. Earlier we separated the world of work into specific functions rather than seeing the whole: HR for hire and fire, flexible working policies and wellbeing; facilities management for workspace, food and beverage, air quality and ergonomics; and IT for the technology that bound us to a desk. But what if we could converge these separate functions into a single entity focused on the experience of work – a group that took a holistic view of how, where and when work takes place in an organization devoid of the rigidity of a formal, hierarchical structure? What if we could use data to create a more flexible workplace?

BY 1911, FREDERICK Taylor was perhaps the world's first management consultant. Inscribed on his tombstone in Pennsylvania are the words 'The Father of Scientific Management'. He believed in optimization and followed in the footsteps of economists such as Adam Smith, with his division of labour, and Henry Ford, whose obsession with specialism led to the automated production line. Fordism and Taylorism set the stage for much of the management thinking of the twentieth century. Taylor was also a Quaker, and, as we have seen, many organizations had their roots in this faith. What is interesting about Quaker worship is that there are no ministers, no hymns, prayers or sermons. Quaker meetings for worship can be held anywhere, at any time. Every meeting begins in silence.

Interestingly, companies such as Amazon, Twitter and the U.S. financial services company Square also start their meetings in silence. Amazon founder Jeff Bezos is renowned for his non-traditional style of management. Rather than the classic 'death by PowerPoint' that afflicts so many meetings, he outlawed 'slide-ware' and would instead start all meetings with the attendees silently reading a narrative for thirty minutes. This memo would describe the context for the discussion to follow, and by tradition the authors' name would never appear on the document; the memo was from the whole team.

Quaker meetings are often arranged with chairs in a circle. As their philosophy states, 'Anyone can contribute to a Quaker meeting for worship – there is no leader . . . and Quaker "business" meetings to organise church affairs are also non-hierarchical and decisions are taken . . . by group consensus.' Their approach echoes many of the ideas in this book, from open-space technology and holacracy to the Team of Teams and busting silos. Perhaps it is no surprise that so many influential organizations were founded by Quakers. With an understanding of more unconventional approaches to organizational theory, we can view the workplace not as a stratified, rigid container, but as an instrument for holding a business in flux – a fluid organization that ebbs and flows, which demands the adaptability we can realize in the twenty-first-century office.

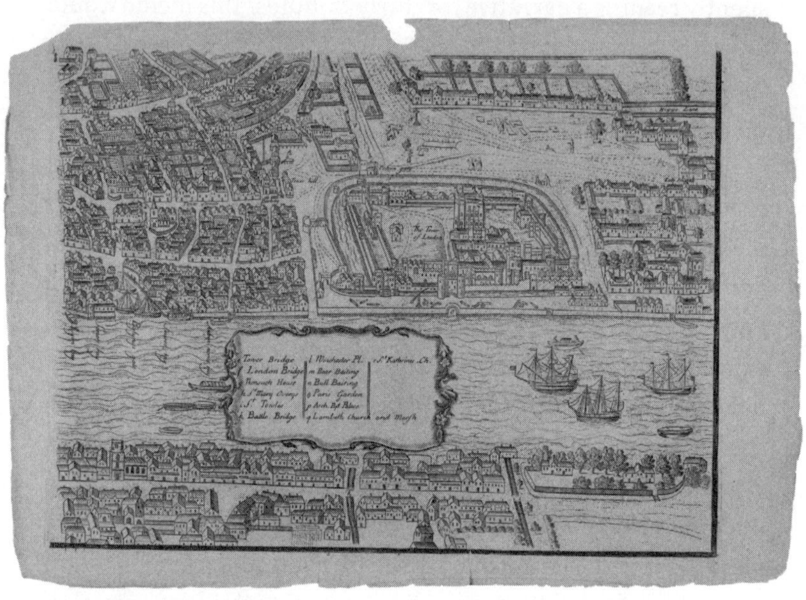

Londinum antiqua, a copy of a 16th-century map of London produced by George Vertue in the 18th century. The city's historic rivers and tributaries shaped the urban plan, in contrast to modern 'grid' cities.

6 Urbanism

The modern office, as it emerged in the early decades of the twentieth century, was rooted in time and place. That place was the city. Since the Industrial Revolution, the urban realm has acted as a magnet for attracting a previously agrarian workforce in the pursuit of wealth, increased earnings and enhanced lifestyles. The advent of clusters of large office buildings brimming with organizational life reflected the economic pull of the city and projected its power. But in the age of virtual technology and a wider distribution of work, why should the city continue to provide a superior approach? In the aftermath of the financial and public health shocks that have rocked our institutions, can the modern city maintain its density to catalyse commerce and stimulate innovation and entrepreneurship?

The relentless pursuit of urbanization has come with a range of challenges. From traffic congestion and poor air quality to pressures on space for living, learning and leisure, as well as a drain on natural resources, the urban realm has been put under pressure. All developed cities suffer from inflated accommodation and transport costs, from shifting demographic challenges and consequent strains on infrastructure, health care and education. Many city leaders and urban planners now talk of a need to 're-boot' the outdated analogue systems of the city and generate a 'City 2.0' to harness emerging digital opportunities.[1]

This analogy to software is not random. In computing, the hardware houses the software, which can be upgraded and re-booted as developments are made. Not so the city – but could we conceive of real estate that has an operating system? One that can be upgraded as needs change? The idea has long been a quest for city planners, as uses change and cities grow. In *How Buildings Learn*, Stewart Brand pointed to the fact that low-cost, standardized, easily modified buildings were the best way to meet changing needs and maintain the economic vibrancy of neighbourhoods and communities. Adaptability now tops the agenda, with its twin cousins of sustainability and reusability high on the list, to create a sustainable future as population growth continues its Malthusian rise.

The inflexibility of our current cityscape contrasts dramatically with where the commercial heart or central business district (CBD) originated. Our medieval cities were shaped on the back of religion and commerce at the intersection of trails and trading routes. The CBD was an exercise in agglomeration – clustering the professions with banking and government was the optimal solution for markets that required face-to-face interaction. The coffee shop became the place for trade and shared information, which subsequently shaped markets such as insurance and inspired the exchanges that evolved as spaces for human interaction.

Our cities have historically been shaped by natural resources and human endeavour. In London, for example, rivers and tributaries of the Thames shaped the urban plan. The River Fleet's valley became Farringdon Road and gave its name to Fleet Street. Marylebone Lane follows the twists and turns of the River

Tyburn. Wells and springs shaped the ancient City such as Brook Street and the gates of the old walled city defined key locations such as Aldgate and Moorgate; this was location in an age where physical rivers marked boundaries and walls created borders.

Urban dwellers created civilization on top of this ancient map. Roman roads followed river beds that are now buried deep below the modern city. Utilities and transport networks overlaid this map to create the mix that we recognize today in cities seen to be attractive and liveable. Their inefficient plan provides the variety and tempo of modern life. In contrast to cities based on an ancient tracery, modern, planned 'grid' cities have a resonance and rhythm through zones, transport planning and a repetitive certainty. This is a Mondrian-style approach to human habitation, within which the tall office towers of the CBD are a distinctive feature. But such cities can sometimes fail to provide a soul.

WHAT HAPPENS NEXT for the city – and for that quintessentially twentieth-century but increasingly dust-blown artefact, the central business district – is now the subject of intense speculation in the aftermath of the global COVID-19 crisis. We predict that a more human-centred city is set to emerge that will move away from this inflexible, rigid approach to planning, zoning and development. The modern city will give way to a mix, or 'intermix', where permeability and interoperability will lead to more fluid and amorphous incarnations of the city plan as boundaries and barriers erode. Property development has long been siloed – commercial, residential, retail and so on. This belongs to an archaic past; a future collision is needed so that we think of our cities as integrated spaces.

Even the 'mixed-use' developments we've become accustomed to seeing haven't got it right yet. Too often, different functions rub along uncomfortably in the same complex, ignoring each other rather than making real connections. We forecast true integration, so that people can work, shop, live, learn and enjoy leisure in the same spaces where infrastructure and amenity is shared – and travel, pollution and environmental impact can be reduced. This concept of 'intermix' sits alongside a call to create more compact cities in which people live closer to work, an idea championed by the World Economic Forum, among others.[2] The advantages of a well-planned compact city include shorter commute times, cleaner air, reduced noise and lower consumption of fossil fuels and energy.

More compact cities comprising a series of intermixed precincts or districts reverse the twentieth-century model of CBDs served by mass commuting from distant suburbs. These new precincts will not only be mixed use – they will be smart. Indeed, digital data and systems will be the glue that ties different uses together. The use of health apps and data-tracking systems adopted in cities from 2020 onwards to combat coronavirus will accelerate the rise of 'digital districts' driven by user data, although concerns over surveillance and privacy – a familiar urban concern – are likely to remain.

City 2.0 will be a more liveable city, more permeable and malleable, so that it adapts with use and provides a stage within which human endeavour can flourish. It will be a throwback to an organic, perhaps inefficient plan that blurs boundaries between work, living, leisure and education and provides a digital overlay so that the city itself balances to the demands and patterns of behaviour of daily life.

Inclusion and community are now central challenges for our cities as the urban realm seeks to create a more egalitarian approach. Suburban and rural fringe communities, traditionally emptied out during the day by commuters, can thrive again as high-net-worth individuals spend time and money in their

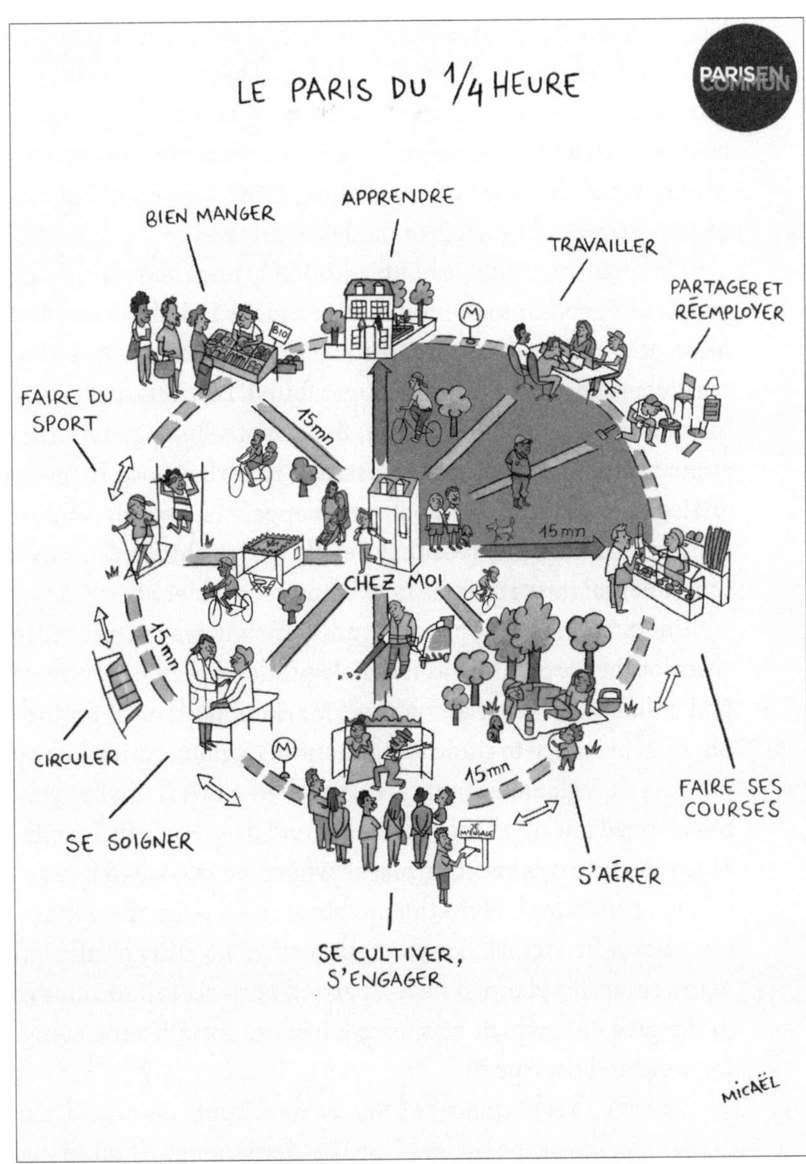

Paris as a '15-minute city' with work, home, shops, entertainment, education and health care all close at hand. More compact cities rewrite the rules of working life. Illustration by Micaël Queiroz, 2020.

local community and not in the CBD. People with special mobility needs and caring roles for children or aged parents are no longer economically inactive as work can be performed locally. Transport infrastructure, long under strain to channel commuters in and out of the heart of cities at the same time each day, can be rebalanced for a different model of demand.

Urban infrastructure has traditionally been about bringing people and goods into the city centre, and the radial pattern that most cities demonstrate creates a heart, a central business district where the commercial hub was found. Districts, nodes and termini create a rhythm of use. But new technology now disrupts this norm. It is safe to assume that the move from an analogue world to a digital one challenges the assumptions of the city plan and the lives that people lead within it. The city's fundamental *raison d'être* is now being reconsidered.

Co-location is no longer the most efficient way to minimize costs for the corporation as technology allows people to connect and collaborate from anywhere. Markets no longer require physical presence to trade and function. Agglomeration has no purpose in a global economy. Distributed work is challenging the planned nature of the metropolis and its spatial efficiencies. Many of the more creative places where we choose to live are less manufactured. Here the medieval town plan, the eclectic streetscape or Victorian asymmetry brings a quality of life that many centrally planned developer-led projects fail to achieve in the grid city, which was once a byword for efficient living, working and transport.

Go back to the squares of Venice or a Cambridge quad, the City of London or the Agora of ancient Rome, and we find spaces and places designed for specific human endeavour, whether the pursuit of learning, commerce or celebration. After the religious buildings, the first commercial structures in the ancient cities of Flanders, Antwerp and London were for the guilds and liveries

– those craftsmen who clustered by skill or trade, by merchant typology for the good of the group. Guilds represented the beginnings of organized commerce, and with each new guild hall, a specific space was meticulously shaped for the various functions of the community: social, training, market and so on. Early guild buildings dominated cities and created the rhythm of commercial life. The architecture was grand and imposing, the signage and iconography descriptive to the profession that was housed.

In Venice, a key centre for commerce and a gateway between East and West, specialist guilds gave way to the *scuole*, organizations that welcomed people from disparate liveries and trades to congregate and exchange ideas. Indeed, the Venetian *scuole* were said to be responsible for the spread of the printed word as early bookbinders and printers mixed with merchants and travellers.

These spaces were grand and imposing, providing places to gather and learn as well as an exchange for those looking for particular skills. Journeymen, the early freelancers or 'gig

Scuola Grande di San Marco and equestrian statue of Bartolomeo Colleoni in Venice, Italy. Wood engraving published in 1884. The *scuola* was an early prototype for the coworking space.

economy' participants in twenty-first-century speak, moved between the guilds of Europe, providing the flow of labour and transference of skills and knowledge. Piecework, or payment for production, was the order of the day, rather than payment for time in the era of employment.

Alongside religious buildings, the guilds and *scuole* dominated early cities. They formed the backbone of the commercial heart of the city before the corporation assumed its mantra as the most efficient mechanism to organize labour and minimize the disintermediation costs of interacting between specialists. Today, we are seeing their re-emergence in a new guise at the heart of trade and commercial endeavour as digital technology challenges the status quo.

As Frances Cairncross predicted in her groundbreaking book *The Death of Distance* (1997), the economics of location have been disrupted by communication technology. The future need for large corporate headquarters to be located in predictable districts within the city centre is now questioned in an age where start-ups can challenge established players with minimal barriers to entry, people can share resources through new cloud-based services and customers can access online marketplaces. Business can bypass the infrastructures of old.

The concept of the corporation as the only entity that represents trade and commerce is now under threat. The predicted rise in the gig economy and the growth of the contingent workforce, an army of specialists and freelancers that sell their time and move between projects and engagements, has implications for the urban realm. In the atomization of the amalgam corporation, we are witnessing the re-emergence of guilds as the coworking movement expands dramatically in cities around the world.

Suddenly, coworking and flexible office space providers have become an influential occupier in major cities, subleasing building after building and using a 'space as a service' model for a community tired of inflexible, stale offices.[3] This model allows space on demand with few constraints and caters to an increasingly peripatetic and agile workforce. Freelancers, start-ups and other independents were early adopters, but large corporates now appreciate the benefits. Coworking spaces provide community, networking and experience, not just desks and meeting rooms. They give people the opportunity to cluster with like-minded coworkers sharing similar skills and attitudes, rather than remaining with the forced camaraderie of corporate life. This is the new guild adapted to an on-demand twenty-first-century model.

AS WE HAVE described, the more that aspects of life become digital, the more location paradigms are turned upside down. The old-school efficiencies of agglomeration, of being close to markets or customers, of having a 'prime location in the central business district' no longer matters in a peripatetic city; this is one based on polycentric properties rather than the old radial infrastructure dictated by river, road or rail and reinforced by politics, power and planning. We have a perfect storm of ingredients to challenge our cities: population growth, transport bottlenecks, carbon-reduction commitments and new technology. Overlay the corporate desire to cut costs and a realization that offices are underutilized assets that can be shrunk to reflect the real demand for workspace and you have a scenario that has the potential to reshape our cities.

The new city set to emerge has no centre or heart but rather a series of interconnected nodes – much like the internet. City 2.0 will be a digital urban landscape, where people and places are connected, with the algorithms of machine learning and AI there to help you make decisions, as nudge takes the place of

Office workers on their lunch break at Broadgate Circle in London. Work and the city are going through a process of renegotiation.

hunch. Ancient, meandering rivers and trails will once again define the most desirable places to be, creating engaging, unexpected and architecturally innovative ingredients for urban renewal.

City 2.0 will redefine how we live, work, commune and consume in the urban realm. As *The Death of Distance* author Frances Cairncross told us in 2020:

> Despite location no longer being critical for certain business decisions, we will still need cities and offices – just not as much as we once thought we did. There is a strength and depth in some big cities that cannot be emulated online, but as people work more frequently from home, urban expectations will turn away from large, dominating business quarters towards more prominent places for entertainment and social activity.[4]

City 2.0 will become a more staccato city, no longer in constant commercial motion but with peaks and troughs as new patterns of behaviour emerge; a doughnut city without a central hub, inhabited by doughnut organizations, as Charles Handy predicted in the 1990s. A polycentric approach will allow new clusters and communities, a new sense of localism and freedom to choose work settings away from the central offices that demand a daily commute and fixed 9-to-5 hours. Overlay onto this the rise of the sharing economy and a vision of autonomous and electric cars, no longer owned and parked most of the time on cluttered streets but ordered via an app on demand, and a new paradigm is inevitable.

We will slowly witness a transformation of our urban landscape as radical and impactful as that created on the back of the first Industrial Revolution. How quickly this will happen depends on specific urban geographies and cultures. What is inescapable

Central Park, New York, built to benefit public health. Urban redesign as an antidote to contagion is nothing new.

is the impetus for change generated by the coronavirus crisis. Fear of disease has often driven change in urban architecture, landscaping and design. Historically, city authorities cleared slums and opened up public spaces in response to the bubonic plague; they widened boulevards and added indoor plumbing to counter yellow fever and cholera.

Green spaces such as Central Park in New York were planned as a direct response to public health concerns; facilities such as Alvar Aalto's Paimio Sanatorium of 1933, designed to treat tuberculosis and other diseases, inspired the streamlined look of modernist buildings and minimalist furniture, which leaves few places for dirt and germs to hide. New urban proposals therefore follow a well-trodden path driven by public health fears.

The economic lockdowns of cities in the early days of the COVID-19 pandemic took cars off the streets and planes out of the skies. As a result, air quality improved and a broad consensus was reached that this was a once-in-a-lifetime opportunity to make changes that will ensure cities become more sustainable. In practice, that has meant challenging the dominance of car travel by widening bicycle lanes to make cycling safer, creating more pedestrian areas and greening the urban realm with 'pocket parks', public seating and other small-scale examples of a trend known as 'tactical urbanism'. All of this will make life different – and better – for workers who will continue to be attracted by the aggregation of people, resources and networks that cities will continue to represent.

7 Space

As the city yields to new pressures and embraces the opportunity to change, so too will the interior working spaces that are so much part of the urban realm. No longer is it important to measure space-planning efficiency by square metres per person in a factory-like container. The office environment is now a destination of choice for company employees who have the option to work remotely, so it must necessarily have more to do with buzz, pull and vibe than with grids, ratios and structure. Space can be inert, leaving people responsible for creating their own ambience, experience and energy, or it can be a vital force, and thus active in shaping their response. The impact of COVID-19 has forced organizations to think more profoundly than ever before about how much space they will need and how they will use it.

The link between architectural form and human behaviour is well documented. If Churchill's famous observation that 'we shape our buildings; thereafter they shape us' is overused, that is because it reflects a universal truth about the influence of space on behaviour.

Interior space in the Interpolis building, Tilberg, the Netherlands, 2003. A pioneering approach to creative activity-based working environments.

Chambers for parliamentary debate not only reflect the political landscape but influence the way politicians behave. Compare and contrast the UK's confrontational debating chamber in the House of Commons, which brings the two-party system directly face to face, with the more collegiate caucus of European assemblies and their horseshoe layouts. Prisons too have studied space as part of the system of managing criminals, going right back to the roundel or 'panopticon model' introduced by the British philosopher and social reformer Jeremy Bentham in the late eighteenth century, which utilized an epicentre as an optimal place to view and control.

The spatial parameters of the modern workplace were set early on during the age of efficiency, limiting the ambitions of designers and funnelling them towards the predictable. There was an obsession with linear and rectangular space as the main topology of the office, with its efficient plan and ease of tessellation fitting into predominantly box-like buildings. While this was fine for the serried ranks of desks in W. H. Leffingwell's utopia of time-and-motion efficiency, we will need something different for tomorrow's knowledge workers.

Many of the default rules adopted by space planners in the modern office are now being questioned. Take, for example, the ubiquitous glass-box rectangular meeting room, where there is just enough room to squeeze around a table and where everyone faces the front to look at a screen or display. These spaces never really engendered the interaction and collaboration required by companies, even less so now. Indeed, they belong in the era before video conferencing took over during the first lockdowns of 2020. Those people not physically present at the meeting appeared in little boxes at the far end of the room on a screen also used for showing the ubiquitous PowerPoint presentation. Anyone trying to connect from a remote location, be it by video or audio, tended to have a poor experience – they were second-class citizens in contrast to those who were present.

But when everyone was forced to work from home, a strange thing occurred. We all became equal – a levelling out happened as nobody was in the office space. Everyone came together on the same platform with the same experience: digital equality was achieved for the first time. Now, as a mixed or hybrid world of work emerges in which some people remain at home and others are back in the office, creating digital equality in meetings becomes more tricky. Anonymous glass-box meeting rooms provided as standard inside offices are not fit for purpose. Instead, we are seeing a host of new technical solutions.

Google, for example, is exploring a range of new spatial typologies that support a blended workforce. Its Campfire technology is an in-the-round space where in-person attendees sit interspersed with large, vertical displays that give remote participants a real physical presence. The displays show the faces of people dialling in at large scale, and directional speakers further enhance the illusion of shared space circled around an imaginary campfire. The circle is widely used in social settings such as therapy and encounter groups, but is much less visible in business ones.

Equality in physical space is indeed an interesting proposition. We should all be equal so that space is allocated by need and not by status, job role, seniority or tenure. Harrison Owen espoused these ideas in his book *Open Space Technology* (1993), where he reflects on the circle as the optimal geometrical shape to encourage community and interaction. Owen based his observations on the anthropology of the West African village of Balamah, which was laid out in a circle with an open space in the middle. 'The circle is the fundamental geometry of open human communication. A circle has no head or foot, no high or low, no

Stanford University's d.school: a space designed to stimulate curiosity and interaction.

sides to take; in a circle people can simply be with each other – face to face.'[1]

Open Space Technology provides a 'methodology for generating ideas and solving problems. It is effective for a diverse group to deal with complex and potentially conflicting material.' The space that Owen suggests to accommodate this process is generous, with people arranged in a circle and coffee and food as a part of the space. Typically, no formal advance agenda is set and people connect, create the schedule and then participate. The process is fascinating and can be seen in other highly innovative spaces that provide an environment for rapid solutions development.

At Stanford University, for example, students from a range of disciplines can join the d.school, a creative unit where they can apply design thinking to innovation challenges.[2] The eclectic space of the d.school is central to this process of ideation: overhead gantries allow moveable panels to be adjusted to create all sorts of tessellations, from enclosed rooms to open settings through to corridors with walls full of ideas. The space is inviting and stimulates surprise and curiosity that drives new types of interaction and learning.

In educational environments, spaces that encourage individual and group learning are now challenging the traditional model of disseminating information to a class in a formal lecture theatre, with the teacher or lecturer facing onto a group of students. Now, a 'flipped' model in which people learn in groups, clustered together at team tables, reverses the normal environment. Formulaic approaches to spatial typology based on efficiency or learned behaviours are being challenged as technology liberates people to work and learn in new ways. Indeed we can learn from other sectors, such as education, that have measured the impact of space on performance.

OVER THE PAST twenty years, in the era of the networked office, there has been growing consensus that the traditional method of allocating one person to one desk, and then providing a few 'break-out' spaces and some meeting rooms, is no longer fit for purpose. When we participated in a global survey of office-space utilization pre-COVID-19 in five industry sectors (finance, government, media, pharmaceuticals and technology), we discovered that average utilization of workstations around the world stood at just 55 per cent; only 43 per cent of conference rooms and just 30 per cent of alternative work settings such as break-out areas were utilized.[3] Much of the workplace was lying idle, yet people reported that they typically couldn't find a meeting room for, say, twelve people, or a project space for a fixed period of time.

Once the pandemic struck, a trend for using office space in a more agile way accelerated. Company leaders realized that people could be just as effective, sometimes more so, when they worked remotely at least some of the time. Presenteeism, a curse of the modern office, was taken off the table by the global pandemic. Surveys of employee opinion suggested that less than one in ten workers wanted to return to 'how it was before', when five days a week were spent commuting to the corporate container. Instead, there was a demand for a new hybrid or blended model of work in which people would divide up the working week between the office, the home and 'in-between' or 'third' spaces such as a café or coworking venue. Company leaders began to calculate what the right formula might be for their organizations – a wrestle with different permutations that continues today and has important implications for managing the corporate space portfolio.

When the Gensler Research Institute, for example, conducted a survey of more than 2,300 U.S. workers in 2020, a majority of office workers said they wanted to return to the office to collaborate with their teams, but not every day.[4] Employees returning to the office also wanted to see 'critical design changes' to reduce density, noise and distraction, which were already affecting performance and satisfaction before the pandemic.

Studies such as this suggest the need for a different space requirement. When the link between people and allocated desks or private offices is broken, a shared model can emerge – one where people can use space as and when they need, much like a hotel where a room is booked for a temporary period and, upon checking out, someone else can then use it. Space can be 'sweated' so that overall occupancy levels rise from around half to a more efficient 80–90 per cent. All of this has the potential to reduce real-estate costs by at least 30 per cent, according to the report 'Reimagining the Office and Work Life after COVID-19', by McKinsey & Co., which states that 'a transformational approach to reinventing offices will be necessary.'[5]

This reduction in costs comes from reimagining what offices are for, what the purpose for travelling into the corporate space is, what activities or tasks are best suited to the office, and who else should be present. Embracing the sharing economy, where people see space as a commodity to be booked and used as needed, provides huge opportunities to challenge the static, conventional office and to provide an appropriate array of work settings. But in recent years, experiments with this approach have disappointed. Many half-baked, ill-considered and badly designed workplaces were anodyne and vacuous – depressing environments with shared or 'choice' seating so that people were assigned a random desk each day. This approach, often called 'hot-desking', derived its name from the Royal Navy, where sailors 'hot bunked' in an environment where space was at a premium. And so people were squeezed in ever-higher densities into a smaller box to save money – a reaction to the cost of real estate and low utilization of offices.

Bland, anonymous and unloved, many 'vanilla solutions' for knowledge workers functioned on the basis of the lowest common denominator – if people were indifferent and didn't actively hate and complain daily about the environment, that was okay with the facilities department. Yet today, companies are not only borrowing from hospitality, but understanding the real work people are doing to align the workplace with activities and teams. Activity-based working (ABW) has emerged as a general descriptor for this progressive approach. ABW was initially based on the premise that work is something you do and not a place you go to, first described by Philip Stone and Robert Luchetti in their seminal 1985 *Harvard Business Review* article 'Your Office Is Where You Are'.[6] It focuses on designing a range of specialist settings based on activities or tasks, equipped with the relevant technology and geared to enhancing experience.

Creatively designed activity-based workplaces, such as the pioneering Interpolis building in Tilburg in the Netherlands, generate a stimulating, adventurous and diverse set of spaces. Interpolis, an insurance company HQ designed by architect Abe Bonnema and updated over three phases between 1996 and 2003, features work by some of the best Dutch artists and designers – Marcel Wanders and Bas van Tol among them.[7] The project was brilliantly conceived and purposefully created to suit people's varied work tasks: there were colourful caves for concentration tasks, brightly lit meeting zones for fast-paced collaboration and large winged chairs for private conversations and contemplation.

The spaces at Interpolis employed a richness of material and colour not normally associated with offices, creating a sense of surprise and amazement. These spaces were based around notional neighbourhoods inhabited by departments or teams sharing communal storage, lockers and micro-kitchens. The

Interpolis philosophy was 'your place of work is wherever you happen to be.' Behind its quirkiness, there was a novel use of space, achieving McKinsey's magic number of a 30 per cent reduction in property costs. Interpolis was a high-profile and successful forerunner for things to come.

IN RECENT YEARS, as the ABW model has become increasingly popular, so its evolution has led to a new vision: activity-based clustering, or ABC. This is our vision for the future, where people sit with like-minded others, in tribes or communities, not based on the organizational chart but on the real work people are undertaking. It uses data, algorithms and AI to create the optimal clusters and experience, and the vision is no longer just theoretical. In Canada, financial service company Scotiabank has implemented an activity-based working initiative called The Way We Work and Where, or W4, based on ecosystems for groups of around five hundred employees based on a common purpose. Scotiabank collected and analysed data in each 'ecosystem' to understand how different groups of people use space and what activities are conducted on a day-to-day basis. More than 7,000 Scotiabank employees drawn from across the organization are now part of the W4 Ecosystem team model. Laura Miller, who leads workplace transformation at Scotiabank, told us: 'We created an outlet where people could have those natural interactions and largely that's going to be one of the things bringing people back into the office . . . we have the tools and technology to enable those interactions.'

As well as what can be observed, a new generation of sensors is entering the physical environment to measure everything, from occupancy to environmental conditions such as temperature or air quality. As part of the revolution known as the Internet of Things (IoT), inanimate objects are being connected to the web and buildings are moving online. Coupled with this move to smart space is a treasure trove of data generated by all the activity that has moved to the cloud. As companies like Microsoft operate Outlook from cloud-based platforms, they can also analyse what is really happening inside the organization. Performance can now be quantified. The top-performing players can be compared to the lower-performing. How many emails are sent each day, how many hours are spent in meetings, the extent of a professional network – all of these things can be measured. Overlay this with occupancy data – what time an employee turns up, where they choose to work, how much coffee they drink – and you have a complete picture of performance of both people and space.

And there's more: dashboards will make recommendations that can shape change and present visualizations of who is emailing whom, and who is being invited to meetings and video conferences. The clusters or tribes that exist in the organization, the informal social networks that flourished in the community office but were not apparent from the official organization chart, will become visible for the first time. Companies have long wondered about how their space is really used and how work gets done. Now they will have the tools to find out. Employees may well, however, have real privacy concerns and so data will be anonymized to present a general picture of the organization rather than single out individuals. But if data can enhance employees' experience, their well-being and perhaps, eventually, allow them to work less as their effort is optimized, we believe they will succumb to greater observation. As we will see in Chapter Thirteen, Generation Z may even embrace this lack of privacy.

People want to work with people. The rush to home working seemed like a good idea and was indeed the only option in the pandemic, but the reality is that good ideas need people to work together creatively. While dispersed teams are fine for focused solo work and acceptable for some limited forms of remote interaction through video, they just don't work for every activity. But to engender learning, to develop new relationships, to catalyse innovation, and to represent the brand and what makes a company unique, physical space is needed. The office needs a vibe: energy and pulse come from proximity and density. The need for speed or velocity in business ensures that decision-making is optimized in an environment where people can get together and make ad-hoc decisions – a contrast to the endless planned or scripted video calls that plague remote workers and constrain progress.

So what is workspace for? Jane Croft, writing for the *Financial Times* in 2020, in the midst of the pandemic, discussed the idea that, for legal firms once occupying swathes of city real estate, 'COVID-19 reinvent[ed] law firm offices as hubs for teamwork and socialising.'[8] The article quotes one firm as announcing a global agile working policy that could see professionals working from home between 20 and 50 per cent of the time. Since then, organizations in many different sectors have stepped forward with their own predictions and models for hybrid working.

We can see a redistribution of office space towards tasks or activities, bonding, relationship building, training, mentoring and interaction, but also towards relaxation and socializing, well-being, health and fitness. The amenities that are often rejected in favour of desk space can re-emerge as the office gets rebalanced based on what people really want and need when they come in. Klaus Sandbiller, who heads global real estate at European bank Unicredit, told us: 'We're recalibrating our office space with less desks, we're looking at multi-functional settings and reconfiguring space for town hall meetings or learning events, and we're exploring the possibilities of using moveable walls and furniture to fit the team size.'[9]

The good news for companies is that alternative space models now exist – and 'third spaces' will be part of the mix along with the office and home. Urban sociologist Ray Oldenburg, in his book *Celebrating the Third Space* (2001), coined the term to define spaces in the community where people get together; a place in between the office and the home.[10] Third spaces borrow from a rich tradition, from the coffee-houses of London or Vienna, where markets such as insurance or scientific exploration emerged, to the modern-day flex-space and coworking versions of the guild or agora. Now these third spaces are in effect becoming part of the workplace, if not the workplace *per se*. The emergence of hybrid working provides for working in between the home and the office building – new spaces that form part of the peripatetic city. As people adopt agile workstyles, they will want a place to work 'on the pause' as they move between home and office.

As well as cafés and bars, these spaces can range from serviced offices to high-end members' clubs. They can be designed in a range of styles, from shabby chic and industrial minimalist to opulent boudoir or classical club, appealing to knowledge workers based on their preferences, location and need. The trend points to another new reality: rather than lease a building for fifteen years and pay for a fixed number of square metres, a company with an agile workforce can occupy less fixed real estate and instead provide a stipend or annual budget to people to 'provision work' through membership of a club. This provides choice and lets people use the workspaces that suit them best. You can select to go to a women-only coworking lounge, such as the Wing in New York, or one devoted to a specific sector, such as the Ministry in London for music industry people.

Guilds and *scuole* – the confraternities that created a place of belonging before the corporation was created – have re-emerged fit for the twenty-first century. Just as the commercial model for technology has been upended, this 'pay-as-you-go' model for space based on membership and use has similarities to the way we now consume software – one that operationalizes the use of real estate and moves it from a fixed to a variable cost.

New attitudes and approaches to workspace will deconstruct some of the most basic parameters around the modern office. We anticipate that spaces will be designed on activity-based principles and be based around clusters – spaces for identified groups or individuals aligned to tasks and activities. Spaces will be designed with a richness and vitality that defines their purpose and 'pulls' people back into the office for specific discrete tasks. With this strategy, companies may well occupy up to 30 per cent less floor space. Combine this with the new urbanism and a more permeable approach with third and in-between spaces, and we have an outline for the way we'll use space in the future.

Comfy, the smartphone app by Siemens, allows workers to books rooms, alter room temperatures and dim or brighten office lights. Digital technology is giving workers the tools to manage their own workplace experience.

8 Technology

Underpinning all the changes to our workspaces, our cities and our organizations is the impact of new digital technology. Digital has changed everything. We've gone from moving paper around to shifting bits and bytes. The medium through which business is shaped and delivered has, for many, become invisible; it is contained somewhere other than the office. The analogue world was easier to comprehend. It was predictable, dominated by objects fixed in time and space. Physical artefacts drove performance and delivered outputs. Work was centred around machinery and equipment, paper and products that provided certainty and stability, and gave working life its rhythm.

The wave of change emerged slowly, but the elements were clear to see. A move of computing power from the central server room, first to the desktop and then the laptop, was the precursor to the idea that we now carry a personal smart 'computer' with us everywhere we go. The death of fixed telephony, Alexander Graham Bell's contribution to mankind in the late nineteenth century, has spawned a revolution in communication: we now expect to call a person, not a place, building, room or desk; to interact with them regardless of location.[1]

The consequences of unbundling distance are profound. While atoms are still expensive to move, bits are now, in effect, free. We have also seen the emergence of the 'cloud', the fluffy name given to the serious business of storing data and processing it in remote centres. Where once the company housed all documents in the office and then housed the servers that housed the documents, now it is anyone's guess where matter is kept. Players such as Amazon power the web by providing storage that is place- or location-agnostic, save for some legal niceties around data privacy.

As computing power has exponentially increased and moved into the hand, handbag and briefcase, as data has become uncoupled from the workplace and as connectivity has become ubiquitous and increasingly unconscious, there is a shift towards a different vision for how, where and when work will take place in the future. In an unconsciously always-on society, the office building as the 'container' for work with fixed hours is no longer relevant. The postal address, telephone number and fax number that allowed communication with physical premises have all become virtual and disconnected to the bricks and mortar that was once the home and hub of corporate technology.

The digital lifestyle of the newest entrants to the workforce, Generation Z (born 1995–2012), informs much of what is to come. Their approach to real-time interaction through platforms such as Snapchat or Fortnite demonstrates an expectation of being connected, always on, interacting synchronously and transparently with their friends. Synchronous interaction – the idea that everything is done together – will become commonplace. Co-authoring, co-creating, co-editing, co-anything will replace the old ways of asynchronous work where documents were passed along the 'production line' in a laborious, sequential process for comment or approval.

The immediacy of camaraderie in a group-orientated game will shape expectations of the office. A gamified workplace will be one consequence of the 'Xbox generation' joining the workforce. Gaming has become a team endeavour, a social platform as much as a competition to win. Likewise, with Snapchat, the experience of instant gratification through exchange of visual messages that evaporate presents a vision of a different world of work – one in stark contrast to the staccato exchange of asynchronous communications in the form of email and text messaging developed and adopted by the Baby Boomers and Generation X cohorts. Their way of working, in largely offline, scripted workplaces, with days full of back-to-back meetings to approve or review documents in stale conference rooms, will be a relic of the past.

In the gamer's world, reality becomes blurred. In physical space, you know where you are; you are influenced and informed by the world around you. Now the digital world is set to augment or replace this reality. Already, using headsets, we can overlay data to enhance what we see or indeed completely replace it in a virtual representation of the real world. These digital spaces can replicate the spaces we want to see or they can create artificial new ones. But the richness of the immersive experience points to the ability to transmute without the need to adapt the environment. Where once people had to travel to experience space and place, now (to a degree) the material world can be delivered digitally.

We have five generations at work today, but it is clear that while Baby Boomers and Gen X did not grow up with the internet, the digital dependants of today are experiencing a different reality. Digital is part of their DNA. The expectations and familiarity of Gen Z with digital platforms will lead to a demand for, and thus a realization, of a digital workplace. This will have a range of attributes that will redefine how and where work is done.

Digital space will be radically different from today's analogue workplace.

A digital workplace is wireless, flexible and mobile, providing choice and diversity to align space and technology to the work people are there to do. Companies want to accelerate process, introduce fast decision-making behaviours and increase velocity. They also need to align workspace to the real work that people are there to do and to growing employee expectations around a healthier low-carbon office. To achieve this, they need digital thinking and a digital workplace.

MEETING MINUTES, accounts files, pitch books and board reports traditionally created reams of paper to be stored in endless metal cabinets. But today all these documents were originated using digital technology, so why print them out and file them? Digital documents that are searchable and accessible are part of a mindset that allows information to be shared and centralized, not stored in filing cabinets or hoarded at a desk. Flexible working that is genuinely independent of place requires that there are no barriers or 'pain points'; access to knowledge, information and working documents needs to become ubiquitous and universal.

Digital documents then require smart devices or displays that provide a 'window' to the cloud where the documents are stored, and these devices and screens can no longer just be anchored to a desk. They need to be mobile and lightweight so that they can be brought into meeting rooms where they then connect and share content wirelessly to surfaces that allow interaction and collaboration. People need to use smart devices during meetings powered by platforms like Zoom or Microsoft Teams; they add to chat, raise a hand or co-create on a digital whiteboard with all content captured as part of the flow of a project. Devices need to be able to be taken to a café or used 'on the pause', in between places while travelling. One of the premises of a digital workplace is that people can connect without plugging in a cable. A 'wireless-first' workplace doesn't mean that there are no cables at all, rather it provides a sense of ease and immediacy for people, allowing them to just be online for most of the tasks they perform at work without having to be tethered.

This all seemed implausible back in 1994, when we published a report titled 'The Cordless Office'.[2] People had never heard of wireless technology, or if they had, they were worried about speed, reliability and security. The office world was obsessed with structured cabling and the networked personal computer (PC). The talk was of cable-managed systems furniture, of raised floors and so-called 'intelligent' buildings. Now cable is dead. People are used to wireless technology – indeed they rely on it; the iPad has no Ethernet port, a smartphone synchronizes with the cloud over wi-fi and 5G wireless networks. The fears over performance, speed and security are now largely gone and people have embraced the flexibility, convenience, choice and mobility that wireless technology brings. Connecting people rather than places or desks, using ever more portable devices and 'unconscious synchronicity', is becoming the new normal.

What is a 'desk'? If we define it as a personal piece of furniture, where an individual's PC, telephone, personal files and Rolodex occupy a 1.2-metre (4 ft) stretch of wood or steel that becomes someone's 'home from home', then, yes, we believe that the desk is dead. With its pedestal full of the paraphernalia of office life – the spare stapler, Cup-a-Soup, company phone directory and an old pair of running shoes – the office desk belongs to a bygone age. It is part of a workplace fit only for analogue battery hens, not the digital, free-range knowledge workers of the twenty-first century.

Gen Z workers will not want a desktop soft toy or picture of their dog pinned to the thin fabric panel that separates them from the human being in the next cubicle. They will want choice and variety. The Schnelle brothers in Germany were right – they were just sixty years too early. Their vision of *Bürolandschaft* set an early blueprint for tomorrow's workplace: a sea of choice with a landscape of workspaces that suit different activities and tasks, personalities and preferences. Surfaces for working on will replace the idea of a 'desk'. As the tethered technology of old gives way to new devices on different platforms, this vision is now taking shape.

The desk was occupied from the 1920s onwards by the telephone and by the QWERTY keyboard, which was first introduced in response to how typists tapped out Morse code and not to slow typists down for fear of the machines jamming, as in popular myth.[3] QWERTY then incongruously survived into the world of word processors and personal computers. The telephone sitting on a desk would be laughable to any Gen Z recruit today. Why would you want to call a piece of furniture and not a person? In fact, why make a phone call at all? Instead, converged or unified communications and collaboration (UCC) platforms are now delivered over the internet from the cloud and accessible through any device; people talking to people, emailing, instant messaging, video conferencing and sharing ideas on platforms such as Slack and Workplace, wherever they are.

As the technologies that once tied people to their desks are removed, one of the barriers to change evaporates. Other technological innovations are emerging to drive change in the way we work and our experience of the workplace. The internet has been transformational for society, but it has largely left physical spaces alone. Now the IoT is set to change the status quo. The foundation is that objects such as light fittings, sensors, switches and locks can be connected by giving them a unique digital address and linking them together on a network. Once they see each other and share data, react and respond to changes in demand and interact with people, a new workplace is possible.

Smart space will emerge to meet the expectations of smart users using smart technology. Connecting the previously unconnected will turn property from a 'dumb container' to a real-time resource. We have termed this trend 'real-time real estate' (or RETRE), and it will begin a transformation of corporate property as data and analytics provide insight into effectiveness, cost and performance – not just of physical assets but of the people that occupy the space.

The idea of a smart building is to create a high-performing workplace where people can interact with their surroundings and each other in new ways. All aspects of infrastructure, from lifts and lighting to the building management system and security, will be smart and 'converged'. New platforms and standards will emerge to unify systems. The creation of location-aware experiences will determine a new type of workplace experience. The IoT will allow inanimate objects to talk to each other.

For some, all of this will sound dystopian. Remember Philip Kerr's 1995 sci-fi novel *Gridiron*, in which an 'intelligent' office building becomes so self-aware that it starts trying to kill everyone inside, confusing real life with a video game? But in this brave new world, environments will know how many people are inside and adjust heating or cooling, lighting or cleaning accordingly to save carbon and cost. Connected devices will generate data and this will be stored in the cloud. Analytics from the 'data lake' that smart buildings will fill gives the facilities team a new role in performance management and a shift towards insight and the ability to 'load balance' buildings.

But the real power that smart spaces will generate is in shaping new experiences and purpose. We all use digital apps in our personal lives, but when we step into the workplace, there is a lack of experience and utility. Much is about to change. We predict that the app-centric workplace will see many of the functions that people need during their working day provisioned through a smartphone app. From accessing the building to finding the way to your meeting, booking a space or requesting a digital locker, ordering food and coffee or checking into a conference room, the app will be the dominant user interface.[4] It will use the location platform enabled by a smart building with technologies such as wi-fi and Bluetooth Low Energy (BLE) beacons to give people a contextualized and personalized experience – the platform will know who you are, your preferences, your real-time location and your calendar.

The latest office developments are already incorporating these technologies more expertly than ever before, for example the state-of-the-art office tower 22 Bishopsgate, in the City of London, which opened in 2021. Developed by Lipton Rogers and AXA Investment Managers at a cost of £500 million, it is billed as Europe's first 'vertical village' and aims to set new standards in design, sustainability and technology integration. AXA's James Goldsmith told us: 'For us, technology is about people's well-being so they can control their environment and it's also to make the building more sustainable.' His colleague Harry Badham added: 'The purpose [of the app] is to make the building feel like any other part of your everyday life. We are not trying to digitize the building and make it digital above all, we are trying to make it human above all and use digital to facilitate this.'[5]

The smartphone is set to be the central node for the future of work, a gateway that is always on and connected to the cloud. It will adapt your experience based on an understanding of personal preferences and circumstances. Workplace apps will help you file expense claims or request holidays; they will plan the logistics for when you come into an office building – where you should sit, with whom and for what purpose. In all of this, AI will make 'informed' recommendations on what you should do, based on historic data analysis of your preferences as well as real-time mining of contextual trends. AI will help shape your working day. It will know what you need to be effective and will direct the right people, resources, spaces and information towards that goal.

Of course, people don't just use their smartphones for work. A blurring of boundaries between corporate apps and personal social media will require new approaches to 'work-life integration', especially for Gen Z. The most forward-thinking companies have resolved issues of security and compliance to allow people to 'bring your own device' to work and use it to access corporate systems. This approach, known as BYOD, democratizes a once autocratic approach to corporate technology. Intel was an early mover in adopting the trend, connecting to an impressive 30,000 mobile employee devices; the software company SAP introduced a special platform to allow employees to use their own devices, although it retained control and the ability to block a device; and asset management giant Blackstone allowed BYOD, but only on Apple products.

BYOD exposes tensions between the type of safe, dull, formal technology that companies have typically provided for employees with the more casual and consumer-friendly tech that people have in their own homes. The general direction is towards a more 'consumerized' workplace, where technology will be less corporate and people will use devices more informally across a range of environments. This line of travel is driven by what companies learned from the global work-from-home experiment during the pandemic regarding giving more choice and flexibility in the provision of technology as a hybrid working model emerges. Adaptation to remote working plays well with those that predict a virtual organization, but people will still need to come together for certain activities. What is clear is that the digital workplace now extends effectively outside the four walls of the office to enable people to work from anywhere.

DATA AND SOCIOMETRICS are set to transform how we measure such things as performance or engagement in the workplace. New ways of mining data from platforms such as Microsoft 365 or Workplace by Meta give insight into patterns of behaviour and effectiveness. Dashboards with real-time and reflective data will allow managers to fine-tune their resources and to measure everything. In the analogue world of the 1920s, frock-coated supervisors watched the backs of people's heads, leading to presenteeism. Today, digital measurement techniques increasingly focus on what people produce – their output rather than the time they sit at a desk.

Technology will also align with a more human-centred approach. While QWERTY dictated the interface between 'man and machine' for a century, new techniques are set to supplant the dexterity of our digits. Voice and touch are emerging technologies that will change the way we interface with devices and systems. Already in the home and on the move, we are becoming used to 'virtual assistants'; the dulcet tones of Siri, Alexa or Cortana have become part of our lives. Now the concept of the voice user interface (VUI) is extending its reach into cars, hotel rooms and the workplace.

We will be able to turn equipment on, start a video conference or order coffee with a voice command, interfacing with the smart systems we described earlier. Increasingly, voice will become the interface of choice, allowing not just control but dictation, transcription and translation of the spoken word. Voice-activated technology will, of course, depend on improving acoustics inside offices; devices won't work properly in noisy environments, so sound-baffling innovations are likely to come to the fore. And just as we have got used to touching the screens of our smartphones and tablets, so haptics will also be important, giving the ability to touch and manipulate data, to move windows on a screen and to bring order to information.

If we can log into our phone or enter a country with our face, the expectation is that we should be able to walk into our office using our biometric identity. The use of facial recognition and similar technologies can also power new experiences and provide a freedom and permeability that people desire at work. The workplace could become as frictionless as possible, without barriers. The COVID-19 imperative to have a contact-free workplace, so as to avoid touching contaminated surfaces, has accelerated company interest in adopting facial recognition.

With smart space and data comes the ability to measure everything. Just as we rate our Uber driver or a hotel stay, so we will start to rate our workplace experience. Whether it's a reception 'meet and greet' or support from a colleague, we are at the start of a gamification of work. People will rate their experiences and score their spaces. A gamified approach produces a workplace in which everything is evaluated – both by the worker and by the employer. Such data can be used to drive improvements in the workplace, but ominously there is also nowhere to hide. Accenture is among the large companies exploring this approach.

IN 2019 MATTHEW TAYLOR, chief executive of the Royal Society for the Encouragement of Arts, Manufactures and Commerce (RSA), presented a set of four technology scenarios from a report by the RSA's Future Work Centre, entitled 'The Four Futures of Work: Coping with Uncertainty in an Age of Radical Technologies'.[6] These scenarios cover a wide spectrum of potential impacts.

'The Big Tech Economy' scenario describes a world 'where most technologies develop at a rapid pace, from self-driving cars to additive manufacturing', but 'unemployment and economic insecurity creep upwards, and the spoils of growth are offshored and concentrated in a handful of U.S. and Chinese tech behemoths.' A doomsday scenario, 'The Exodus Economy', describes an economic slowdown and a crash on the scale of 2008, keeping workers trapped in a low-skill, low-productivity and low-pay cul-de-sac; a scenario called 'The Empathy Economy' offers a more positive future:

> Technology advances at a clip, but so too does public awareness of its dangers. Tech companies self-regulate to stem concerns and work hand in hand with external stakeholders to create new products that work on everyone's terms. Automation takes place at a modest scale but is carefully managed in partnership with workers and unions.

Disposable income in a time of high employment flows into 'empathy sectors' like education, care and entertainment.

'The Precision Economy' is of particular interest. This portrays 'a future of hyper-surveillance . . . Technological progress is moderate, but a proliferation of sensors allows firms to create value by capturing and analysing more information on objects, people and the environment. Gig platforms take on more prominence and rating systems become pervasive in the workplace.' The RSA report continues:

> While some lament these trends as invasive, removing agency from workers and creating overly competitive workplace cultures, others believe they have ushered in a more meritocratic society where effort is more generously rewarded. A hyper connected society also leads to wider positive spill overs, with less waste as fewer resources are left idle.

This, we believe, is where an optimized, data-driven workplace is heading. It conjures a vision of real-time real-estate cutting costs (energy, food waste, underutilized space) while improving experience (service, support, connections). Machine learning and AI, predictive analytics and sociometrics will further transform the world of work. Workplace apps that are 'location aware' will change the user experience and provide enhanced productivity by aligning space with preference and activity, while directing social networks in buildings to accelerate serendipity. Are we ready for such precision? Can we cope with it?

Public gallery on the 10th floor of the OPPO headquarters, Shenzhen, China. Visualization by Zaha Hadid Architects, 2020.

9 Designing

'Have you ever stopped for a moment to think about your workplace? Who designed it and why? Who laid out the corridors? Who planned the number of desks there would be, or the siting of the amenities?' Andy Law, former CEO of the London-based advertising agency St Luke's, asked these questions in his book *Open Minds*, published in 1999, which discussed the agency's radical office design where people didn't have a desk and instead the workspace was given over to their clients. 'Each client had its own purpose-built creative communications centre and the owners of St Luke's (all staff were shareholders) had what was left – the open spaces, the restaurant spaces, the crazy spaces. We disposed with personal desks altogether.'[1]

St Luke's is important to understanding what comes next in designing because its office space was created to reflect its people, the spirit of its culture, the work being done and the energy of the process – it was not trying to conform to any standard model of smooth business professionalism. As Law reflected: 'All offices are the same. They are brick and glass edifices, either purpose-built or redeveloped, full of conduits for cable, and neatly squared-off working zones. Most are like a graceful swan – elegant, smart, purposeful and well preened. We are an upside-down swan and the untidiness is part of the flapping feet that are on full display.'[2]

The St Luke's office was an early pioneer of creative workplaces that owe more to the slightly chaotic 'fail fast' mantra of the start-up than the Six Sigma doctrine of corporate perfecionism in project management. During its heady days in the 1990s, it offered an alternative to workplace architects and designers frustrated with the formulaic constraints of their trade. Designing offices today is a practice with a much wider vista of opportunity, and one of the reasons why this should be so is the rich potential of data to inform the design process itself. The design professions are still on the foothills of fully understanding the relationship between data science and design of the physical work environment, but things are starting to move fast, and we predict a growing relationship between designing and data science to create better workplaces for the future.

Designers have always used various types of information to create new workplaces. The hierarchical 'org chart' familiar in Taylorist offices was used to determine headcount, the number of desks, the adjacencies of different departments (who should sit near whom) and the specification of furnishings and finishes based on corporate rank and status. Later, observations, interviews and space-utilization studies were introduced to create a richer picture. This approach included some in-depth ethnographic research as the HR discipline gained more traction in companies. But much of the data produced to guide design decisions was subjective and restricted in scale, due to the limited ways that human activity in the office environment could be measured.

Today, however, new data tools with cutting-edge sensor technologies can scientifically reveal the deeper patterns of interaction, communication and team dynamics within the workplace. Metrics around collaboration that were intangible before are now within the grasp of employers. In the past, observational data was integral to understanding how people connect and communicate. But not all communication is visible. Analysis of email, calendar and meeting-booking data, and the use of sociometric badges worn by employees that anonymously measure face-to-face interaction through embedded proximity sensors, bring these exchanges into the open for the first time.

When applied to office design, objective quantitative measurement of what's really happening in the workspace means that companies can experiment and discover interesting relationships between different variables, such as re-siting coffee points or rearranging furniture, lighting and partitions. Once a large data lake has been collected, organizations can use AI and machine learning to predict patterns of interaction and communication.

Zaha Hadid Architects has been among the leading design firms pioneering this new avenue. In a development it terms 'the self-learning workplace', the design firm believes that environmental and occupancy data collected from sensors will play a growing role in reshaping workplace design. It is now using algorithms to model complex dynamic networks within large Chinese offices with massive floor spaces, achieving different spatial configurations in seconds that would once have taken an architectural studio thousands of man hours to do. Ulrich Blum, senior associate at Zaha Hadid Architects, told us:

> Digital tools give greater insight into how and where we should work. We've developed an algorithm that enhances the design process – it looks at connectivity from a distance and visual perspective and identifies the desks which have optimum communication potential. A company can then use this information to sit the

right people in these spaces to optimize innovation and knowledge sharing within the organization.[3]

New workplaces were once designed to a point of frozen architectural perfection whereupon the scheme would be professionally photographed, often before the workforce arrived to mess it up, and the designer's work would be considered done. Today, workplaces are in what design professionals describe as 'a constant state of beta' – a bit like what St Luke's was trying to achieve in the 1990s. This permanently temporary approach will lead to an evolving and continuous relationship between companies and their designers, as changes are constantly researched, modelled and adjusted using data gathered on a real-time basis.

ANOTHER EMERGING FACET of designing that we are likely to see is the growing use of participatory design or co-design in the workplace, as employees do not have offices designed *for* them but designed *with* them. Modern offices were shaped largely through commercial design briefs being given by senior managers to architects and consultants. If there was any employee input, it tended to be through a consultative committee that was often there for show and could easily be ignored. Co-design processes, in which office workers are equal participants in a relocation or a refurbishment, have been relatively slow to catch on in the workplace. This is despite the prominent role of workplace councils and unions in shaping the contours of the social democratic office in Northern Europe in the post-war era; and in contrast to the steady adoption of co-design in other areas such as neighbourhood development or public service provision.

Research suggests that giving employees more control over the design of their workplace by bringing them into the process makes a positive contribution to their well-being. A UK study by the Royal College of Art with architectural firm Gensler discovered that an invitation to participate in designing the work environment raised levels of well-being,[4] although increasing the level of participation from low to high did not necessarily increase them further. Inviting employees into the design process is part of a wider strategy to adapt space to suit user needs, rather than fit people into standard design concepts.

It can also be a tool to build company culture. When online retailer Zappos moved into an abandoned city hall in downtown Las Vegas, it did not turn the blank space over to interior designers but instead encouraged its own people to design and decorate the building as they saw fit. In 2015, Melbourne-based ANZ Bank introduced a pioneering series of modular and moveable elements called Playbox so that its employees could reconfigure their team spaces as they wished. This mobile kit-of-parts concept reduced the time and cost of fitting out a typical office floor in the bank while significantly improving staff engagement. The Playbox enabled desks to be 'daisy chained' together, and walls, lockers and furniture to be moved. All the elements could be packed away and fitted in a goods lift to be transferred between floors. As ANZ Bank's head of workplace, Ken Lynch, told us: 'Codesigning with the business, we were able to generate better returns than we've seen before. Staff engagement increased from 30 per cent to 90 per cent in some cases just by asking the staff to design the space themselves through the kit of parts.'[5]

Teams tend to know best how they want to work, and how different office elements should be arranged. Historically, they simply have not had a voice. Amazon was famous for its original 'door desk'. Back in 1995, as the business grew, employee number five, Nico Lovejoy, suggested a visit to the Home Depot store across the street. They ended up making their own desks from doors that were cheaper than the desks on sale, and so a necessarily efficient solution ended up as part of Amazon folklore. The do-it-yourself desk became a distinctive part of the culture, and thousands of Amazon employees still work on modern versions of the original door desk. Meeting rooms are also equipped with folding tables more at home at a DIY store. Today Amazon recognizes ideas that deliver lower prices to customers with the Door Desk Award.

While we are likely to see more employee-initiated design ideas in the workplace in the future, leading to less orderly and more eclectic environments generally, companies will not hand over control completely. Designers will continue to be asked to create spaces and settings which engender certain behaviours in the workforce that can be beneficial to the organization. One of these is bringing people together in random and serendipitous encounters to encourage collaboration and innovation, the so-called 'bump' factor. Before COVID-19, this was becoming a must-have on most office design briefs. Even after the social distancing protocols of the pandemic briefly curbed enthusiasm for the chance encounter, the 'watercooler' moment remains part of office folklore.

The origins of this approach lie in the legendary Building 20 at the Massachusetts Institute of Technology (MIT). Built in 1943, it spawned a whole host of post-war technological breakthroughs (from radar to microwave technology) due to a flexible design promoting spontaneous collaboration. Famous for being a shabby space for temporary demand, it allowed people to adapt and hack the environment. Walls and floors could be removed, equipment installed and the radical 'plywood palace' ensured that the space was not precious. Known as 'the magical incubator', Building 20 assumed almost mythological status among designers and developers who tried to emulate its approach.

In the late 1950s, Bell Labs' research facility in Murray Hill, New Jersey, designed by Eero Saarinen to house more than 6,000 engineers and researchers, adopted a similar approach: its offices were spread along far-reaching corridors to ensure staff would bump into each other as they moved through the labs. The invention of solar cells and transistors resulted from these collaborations. If you compare MIT's Building 20 and Bell Labs at Murray Hill with the proscribed circulation routes and departmental silos of companies operating in standard office blocks, then you might imagine why using design to orchestrate chance encounters has real appeal for business leaders. The example of Sony's failure to see the coming of the iPod shows that separation can have a disastrous effect. Indeed the space planners' obsession with adjacency – putting groups or departments together because the org chart tells them to – flies in the face of a company that wants to engender chance encounters. Here dis-adjacency makes more sense; a randomness and inefficiency that encourages the meanders that create the unexpected conversations.

Companies are today combining design with technology, using data analytics and digital apps to bring people together, but architectural interventions remain important. For example, the punching of giant social staircases through several floor slabs, opening up the organization for cross-departmental and cross-disciplinary collaboration, has become a recurring feature of various workplace schemes. In London, for example, Macquarie Bank at Ropemaker Place and Adobe at the White Collar Factory have both made spectacular insertions into their workplace to promote casual collisions – the stairs descending and ascending between floors seeming to defy architectural logic.

Connective staircases also feature strongly in Boston Consulting Group's New York office at Hudson Yards, where the company has even developed a 'collision coefficient' to measure the number of encounters, encourage people to move around and recommend colleagues to meet within the workforce. This scientific metric is derived and then applied by use of technology

Social staircase in Boston Consulting Group's office at Hudson Yards, New York, 2017. The company piloted a 'collision coefficient' to measure interactions.

(sociometric badges, sensors and apps); in a first for office design, collisions are engineered by both architectural and technical means.

ONE OF THE challenges of a hybrid work model where people are no longer present in the office every day is bringing the right people together at the right time to collaborate. The fewer people in the workplace, the less chance of the random encounter that can lead to innovation. While some interactions are transactional or formal, others are creative and driven by the need for ideas. Innovation can be compared to a game of snakes and ladders. Many new ideas are the result of sequential endeavour, plodding along methodically from square to square. Sometimes people have a eureka moment and jump ahead by scaling the ladder. All too often developments hit a snake and we fall backwards – the 'fail fast' culture of Silicon Valley dusts us off and sets us back in the game.

Snakes and ladders originates from an ancient Indian board game, originally known as Moksha Patam, and was closely linked to the concept of karma or destiny in Hindu philosophy. And so, the analogy of the uncertain path or journey is one that resonates with the approach to creating spaces for innovation. They can't be linear and predictable in a world where good ideas arise from the unexpected. Meanders, surprise and the unplanned path are design ingredients in a workplace that wants to engender radical ideas and alternative approaches.

The office needs a level of unpredictability if its aim is to incubate new ideas and push boundaries. But some cultures, such as the traditional Japanese workplace, are at odds with the randomness that is being suggested. When Geert Hofstede analysed employees at IBM across forty countries, he found distinctive differences. Japanese employees were far more collectivist compared to the individualism demonstrated by what he defined as the 'Anglo-Saxon' block. His findings, published in *Culture's Consequences* (2003), point to a cultural dimension to workspace. Hofstede measured, for example, uncertainty avoidance, and found again that Japanese culture was higher on the scale than older democracies like the UK or the Netherlands. High uncertainty avoidance cultures are more dogmatic, authoritarian and traditional, shaping a predictable workplace that can provide more control.

Volatility and 'random walks' are hard to manage but more reflective of real life; how we model market movements, migrating birds or the random fluctuations of Brownian motion appear inexplicable, but follow a mathematical model. Uncertainty is baked into much management thinking. In *The Black Swan*, Nicholas Taleb's 2007 best-selling treatise on the impact of rare and unpredictable outlier events, Taleb talks of low predictability but high impact: 'Black Swan logic makes what you don't know far more relevant than what you do know.'[6]

So, the unexpected could have a significant role in future workplace design. Ideas might range from installations by artists-in-residence to changes in physical space made overnight in order to surprise and delight, or to a user-defined workplace where employees themselves can shape and adjust their surroundings. All of these design strategies point to a different approach that triggers different behaviours and generates Black Swan thinking.

Walt Disney was famous for putting people's work in progress on display overnight so their ideas and concepts were there for all to see as they arrived at work the next morning – people could react, comment, be inspired and help the development of creativity. Much the same approach was adopted at IDEO, one of the world's leading design and innovation firms, resulting in employee-designed studio space in Silicon Valley decorated with hanging bicycles and half-finished prototypes. As IDEO co-founder David Kelley notes: 'It might look like chaos but it's focused chaos. The general principle with work environments at IDEO is to try stuff and then ask for forgiveness, rather than ask for permission first.'[7]

In the MIT Media Lab in Boston, where numerous chalkboards punctuate the space, people sit and brainstorm in the open, and then leave their scribblings and musings on the board for all to see with their contact details – people can add their own insight or connect with the brains behind the knowledge. This approach to 'displayed knowledge' aligns design with organizational culture. Instead of planning ratios of desks and meeting rooms scaled by headcount, designers are now required to create spaces with latent memory – to help team members build on each other's ideas in an act of collective endeavour.

IN THE SEARCH to make organizations more innovative, workplace design has become skilled in recent years in bringing the outside in. Biophilia, entrance-level cafés, food courts, exhibition space, public viewing platforms and other elements have entered the interior mix to make the office feel part of something bigger. But today the focus is on taking the inside out – about connecting the workplace to the neighbouring district as part of an ecosystem of collaborative innovation. It's no longer enough to design the office interior with social staircases for random encounters and pin-up spaces for displayed knowledge. It's just as important that employees have direct access to external public and cultural amenities, transport links, university research, entrepreneurs and start-ups, restaurants and retail. Even the restrictions imposed by the global pandemic won't alter that belief.

The emergence of the innovation district as a wider frame for workplace design owes something to generational change and the rise of the millennial workforce, which tends to see the workplace as more than just a desk in the office. Instead, the millennial workplace extends beyond the office walls into the neighbourhood and the wider city. An emphasis on the scale of the district as opposed to the office plan is also a product of how innovation itself is changing.[8]

No longer do large organizations depend entirely on internal resources to innovate; the fortress-like corporate R&D lab guarded by men in white coats is now being replaced by more permeable and networked innovation settings, which are more open to collaboration with a range of external parties. The term 'collaborative innovation' is itself often interchangeable with 'open innovation'. It refers to a process in which multiple players both inside and outside an organization contribute towards the development of new products, services and business solutions, and openly share what they develop. And you can't do that from behind the closed doors of the corporate office.

Apple's decision to support the launch of the iPhone by inviting thousands of external software developers to create applications for its new device, and share them online through the App Store, is a good demonstration of how collaborative innovation works. The whole idea is to enable large businesses to link their scale and resources with the ideas and agility of start-ups and specialists. Against this background, locating your business in an innovation district where the right connections can be made with diverse partners, begins to make sense.

Of course, you can practise collaborative innovation at different scales. Many companies, Visa, Microsoft and IKEA among them, continue to favour internal innovation labs that are contained; this is because access, ideas and IP can be controlled more

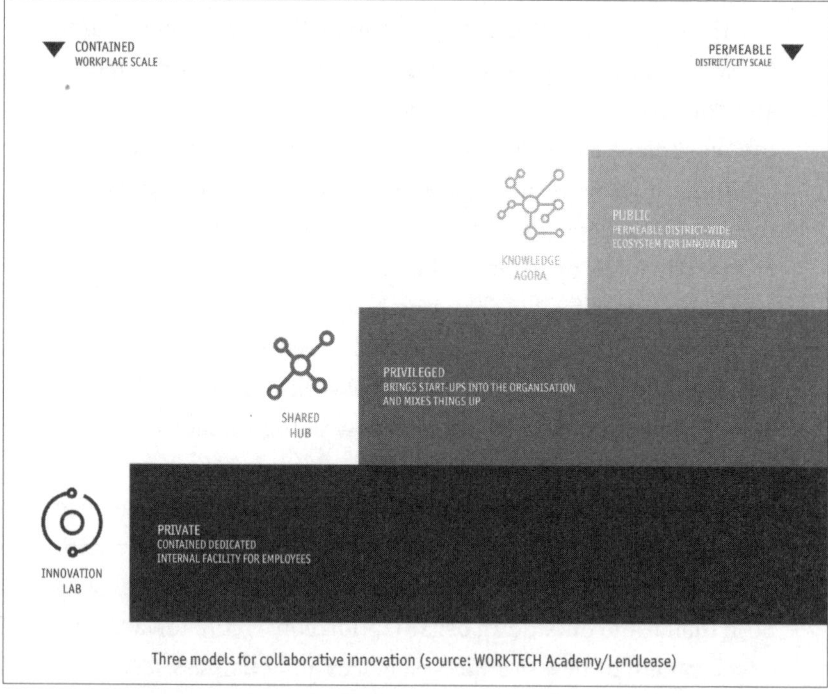

Three models of collaborative innovation – from private and privileged to public. Worktech Academy/Lendlease (2018).

easily. But these spaces increasingly depart from the old R&D labs by having a more social vibe and a new design flavour with agile scrums, quiet zones and project rooms – and they involve a wider range of innovation partners than just colleagues.

At a more permeable scale are shared hubs designed for collaborative innovation, which bring start-ups into the corporate organization, effectively through a joint venture. This approach is popular in the financial services industry where Barclays and Natwest have used the model to collaborate with fintech disruptors. The shared hub also allows companies to co-create with customers and university spinouts – its design elements include member lounges, active lobbies, coworking zones, immersive exhibitions, incubators and boot camps.

The most permeable model for collaborative innovation is the district scale. It is here that the organization can connect with research centres, maker spaces, meeting spaces and other outsourced innovation services, within a dynamic, convivial and practical business landscape offering a strong hospitality dimension. Many examples of the innovation district, or what we term the twenty-first-century 'knowledge agora', now exist from King's Cross or Stratford in London to Biopolis at One North in Singapore.

As the innovation lab is ostensibly private, the shared hub is privileged and the innovation district is public, designers will be required to think in new ways to help organizations to innovate. In the future, the ability to model space and amenities in complex patterns across a range of scales will increasingly rely on the digital tools and datasets that we have described in this chapter. Can we see a future in which design studios will swap out their materials libraries for data libraries? As the modern office is reimagined, so too will be the process of designing.

The Spheres, biodomes at Amazon's Seattle headquarters, designed by NBBJ. The trio of spherical conservatories opened in 2018 and house 40,000 plants, providing a green retreat for staff.

10 Diversity

Talk of diversity in the workplace was originally a consequence of discrimination. Equal opportunities reinforced by legislation directed employers not to recruit with any bias towards race, gender, age, sexual orientation, religion, ethnicity, language, education or ability. Today, diversity has a deeper and more compelling meaning – it brings a whole new point of difference to the organization. But do companies realize the benefits of having a more diverse workforce?

A rebalancing with historically under-represented groups can be symbolic, but successful companies succeed by employing diversity as a core value. Mixing human capital produces results. Research points to enhanced performance and improvements realized by diverse teams, boards of directors and partnerships because people bring different views, backgrounds, experiences and perspectives.

Many organizations today try to recruit not in their own image but with an approach that attracts talent from different backgrounds. But when these diverse individuals enter the workplace they are often squeezed into a homogenous box where one size fits all. Uniformity and consistency trump variety and choice in a workplace modelled around a common denominator to which people must adjust. Fitting 'square pegs into round holes' may sit easily with a lazy approach to space planning and design, but organizations that celebrate diversity need to provide more options. People want to better align themselves with spaces in which they feel comfortable in order to perform to their optimum level. And they need experiences aligned to who they are as much as what they are trying to do.

Personality and psychometrics have a part to play. Carl Jung defined the foundations of personality in his 1921 book *Psychological Types*, arguing that people have fundamental differences.[1] His view of introversion and extroversion established the notion that we can define people by characteristics and set in motion the study of human typologies. In the 1950s Isabel Myers and Katharine Briggs built on Jung's work to develop a set of tools based on tests that profiled sixteen different types of action. Myers–Briggs demonstrated that humans have distinct personality types or temperaments, and despite their familiarity, these tools remain relevant today.

The Dionysian temperament (or SP in the Myers–Briggs taxonomy) defines a person who loves freedom, who is action-orientated and impulsive, a free spirit who becomes bored with the status quo. They like to vary their work patterns every day, to try out new things and to be spontaneous. SPs would have a particular preference for workspaces that would be very different to others. Prometheans (NT in Myer–Briggs) meanwhile focus on the future and are architects of change. They blur work and life and are perfectionists and visionary leaders. Their preferred workplace is collaborative and energized, with spaces to share and explore ideas, to solve problems and build models.

Compare this to the Epimetheans (SJ in Myers–Briggs) who like to belong. They are often members of clubs or churches; family is important, and they maintain continuity and enjoy routine. Classic jobs are teachers, managers or administrators, and they bring stability to an organization. Their preferred workplace is more ordered and traditional: they like to go to the same space each day, enjoy a sense of belonging, and like order and familiarity. The sixteen key variants point to diversity in who we are and how we like to work. In different spaces, one type will thrive and enjoy interaction while another will feel drained and find it impossible to work productively.

Academic studies have reinforced these assumptions. The work of F. S. Morgenstern, R. J. Hodgson and L. Law, published in 1974, found that 'it would seem that the extraverted subjects do not merely prefer to be in the company of others, but that their work efficiency actually improves in the face of distractions, while the solitary preferences of the introverts are reflected in their reduced efficiency of work when distracted.'[2] As Cal Newport suggests in his book *Deep Work* (2016), to produce at your peak level you need to work for extended periods with full concentration on a single task free from distraction.[3] This contrasts to 'shallow work', which is plagued by the distractions of the digital world and the visual and acoustic interruptions of the modern workplace.

Newport built on the work of the psychologist Mihaly Csikszentmihalyi, whose book *Flow* (2002) talked of the need for uninterrupted time to complete creative tasks.[4] Csikszentmihalyi used experience sampling as a technique to measure the impact of the unexpected on concentration. A state of 'flow' – an 'optimal experience' of creative enjoyment and total involvement with certain types of work – required deep concentration with uninterrupted periods of time of say eighteen to twenty minutes to achieve this state. And he discovered that people were happier at work than at leisure if they realized 'flow'.

In Susan Cain's seminal book *Quiet: The Power of Introverts in a World that Can't Stop Talking* (2012), she described 'New

Groupthink' and the focus on teamwork in the modern workplace: 'Today's employees inhabit open office plans, in which no one has a room of his or her own, the only walls are the ones holding up the building, and senior executives operate from the centre of the boundary-less floor along with everyone else.' Cain is not a fan of open-plan workplaces that 'have been found to reduce productivity and impair memory. They're associated with high staff turnover. They make people sick, hostile, unmotivated, and insecure.'[5]

Cain's view is that personal space is vital to creativity and she suggests that many writers, thinkers, designers and artists do their best work from secluded studies or studios. But she also recognizes that 'face-to-face interactions create trust in a way that online interactions can't. Research also suggests that population density is correlated with innovation; despite the advantages of quiet walks in the woods, people in crowded cities benefit from the web of interactions that urban life offers.' She admits that she couldn't have written her book alone in her home office. 'I wrote this book on a laptop at my favourite densely packed neighbourhood café. I did this for exactly the reasons that champions of the New Groupthink might suggest: the mere presence of other people helped my mind to make associative leaps.'[6]

Cain concludes that 'we need to create settings in which people are free to circulate in a shifting kaleidoscope of interactions, and to disappear into their private workspaces when they want to focus and be alone.'[7] This reinforces the view that we have explored in this book: employees thrive in a heterogeneous workplace, and it is time to give up the homogenous approach of the old modern office. Diversity in all its forms is therefore critical to this goal.

Many others have reflected on the influence of place for creativity. J. K. Rowling famously booked herself into a suite at Edinburgh's Balmoral Hotel – a place devoid of the distractions of her home office – to finish the final volume in the Harry Potter series, *Deathly Hallows*. Bill Gates was known to take a week out each year for thinking; he hibernated in his cabin with books for inspiration. Changing settings, inspiring vistas, peace and quiet, calm and solitude all seem to point towards creative endeavour. But here lies a contradiction, as there is also a belief in the mantra that creativity comes from collective endeavour, interaction and collaboration.

There is a philosophical tension between the solo state of uninterrupted 'flow' to spark ideas and the bustling teamwork of many innovative companies – the tech workspaces of Silicon Valley are inhabited by engineers sharing vast open floorplates, where the ability to share ideas, to eavesdrop and learn by osmosis, to co-create and collaborate is easily and purposefully enabled. The organization that is truly diverse will design offices that cater to both types of work. Building 20 at MIT in Boston was a successful wartime solution to house scientists from eclectic backgrounds and industries. Its message today is clear: hackable spaces that allow people of diverse backgrounds and talents to adapt and personalize their working environment will lead to innovation. Hackable spaces evade the dead hand of regulated facilities management.

AMID GROWING FOCUS on such issues as Black Lives Matter, the gender pay gap and greater recognition for neurodiverse people in the workplace, there is a body of academic study that shows multicultural organizations are more successful than those defined as monolithic or plural. Research suggests that diversity increases creativity and performance, although there are also downsides. As diversity increases, consensus diverges owing to the many different viewpoints and perspectives, and it can be harder to unite people and agree on a common purpose. In their article for the *Harvard Business Review*, 'Teams Solve Problems Faster When They're More Cognitively Diverse', Alison Reynolds and David Lewis discuss their findings that group diversity in terms of age, ethnicity and gender does not correlate to an increase in performance.[8] It is cognitive diversity – how individuals think – that provides a more intriguing insight.

The upsides of cognitive diversity in terms of innovating are now bringing neurodiverse employees in from the cold. Not so long ago, people with such conditions as autism, dyspraxia, dyslexia and ADHD (attention deficit hyperactivity disorder) struggled in the workplace. Employers were often slow and reluctant to make the necessary adaptations for neurodiverse minds – or even recruit them in the first place. Today the situation is changing: there is growing appreciation that people and ideas from outside the boundaries of neurotypical thinking have a great deal to contribute to company breakthroughs. According to the *Harvard Business Review*, 'research shows that some conditions, including autism and dyslexia, can bestow special skills in pattern recognition, memory, or mathematics.' Many people with dyslexia exhibit unusually strong visual and problem-solving skills; ADHD workers can be hugely creative, dedicated and energetic, with a strong ability to think outside the box. Commentators have noted how many successful people working in science and engineering jobs on innovation tasks have neurodiverse traits.

The term 'neurodiversity', first coined in 1998 by the Australian sociologist Judy Singer, has itself come of age in the workplace. Not before time, one might add, as one in ten full-time office workers are considered to be neurodiverse, according to some estimates. So, what do neurodiverse people struggle with in the working environment? Bright lights and background noise would be a fair summary. Distractions are a huge problem for these members of a workforce, so companies are now looking at designing spaces with areas for focus and escape, away from constantly being pinged by technology.

Companies often recruit in their own image. But this can result in functional bias and low cognitive diversity. To deal with uncertainty and complexity, they need to encourage different thinking, and create a safe environment for people to experiment and try to solve problems in different ways. In Edward de Bono's *Six Thinking Hats*, the father of lateral thinking describes diversity of thought generated by diversity of behaviour.[9] Through parallel thinking, he defines six different-coloured hats to represent different directions of thinking.

In contrast to the psychometric types of Jung and Myers–Briggs, de Bono adopts a Confucian approach, based on behaviour and not personality. Each colour represents a function that switches the way people think: white for objectivity through facts and figures; red for emotion; black, sombre and serious to find weaknesses; yellow for optimism and positive thinking; green for creativity and new ideas; blue for control and the organization of the thinking process. This approach begs the question: does today's workplace encourage cognitive diversity? We suggest not. In all but the most progressive offices, a continued reliance on bland, repetitive arrangements of desks and meeting rooms define predictability and are the antithesis of the unexpected.

At the extreme of organizational diversity is a collection of individuals. So, should we not seek to understand each individual so that they can produce their best work? Peter Sole, a change management thinker, said 'organizations don't change, people change. Organizations change in units of one.'[10] McKinsey & Co. research points to the benefits of diversity in leadership teams.[11] Its study of 180 publicly traded companies in France, Germany, the UK and the USA found that in companies ranking in the top quartile of executive-board diversity, returns on equity were 53 per cent higher and earnings before interest and taxes were 14 per cent higher, on average. The board diversity in question was measured by the number of women and foreign nationals in senior positions, particularly those who seemed to play critical roles in the companies and who were involved in making key decisions, including risk taking.

The link between diversity and the willingness of organizations to take risks is a common theme. But the workplace has some deep-rooted barriers to risk-taking, based on structures of power, conformity and control. In her book *Open Plan* (2020), design historian Jennifer Kaufmann-Buhler explains how the original ideals for open-office space in the 1960s – to create a more egalitarian society – were lost in the decades that followed. Open plan mutated into the corporate 'cube farm' and the needs of white able-bodied male professionals were constantly prioritized over those of women, people of colour and workers with disabilities. According to Kaufmann-Buhler, 'Open plan was never a place in which all workers and all positions were treated or even imagined as equal.'[12]

Although the development of the American open-plan office in the early 1960s was roughly concurrent with the country's civil rights movement, a legacy of racial segregation and discrimination hung over the U.S. workplace long after the Jim Crow laws were history. Kaufmann-Buhler notes that Black Americans were held back, along with Latinos and Hispanics, and other minorities. In open-plan space, women were repeatedly ogled at and propositioned; disabled people in wheelchairs were unable to peer over partitions; and LGBTQ+ workers felt exposed and pressured to 'mask their identities through performative heteronormative and heterosexual behaviors and interactions'.[13]

TODAY, ONE OF the ways in which firms can achieve diversity is to encourage more chance encounters. As the antithesis of 'like attracts like', diversity in action has to drive unexpected interactions, the unplanned encounters that lead to diverse thinking and outcomes. The 'water cooler moment' can generate new ideas in a non-scripted office. The underlying principle is that ideas are generated from the 'adjacent possible' – those unexpected moments. So, can we design a workplace that engineers serendipity and creates the unplanned opportunities for diverse employees to interact?

Bringing diverse ideas into random collision in the workplace is essential, as we have described previously. Steven Johnson's book *Where Good Ideas Come From* (2010) describes the 'adjacent possible' that biologist Stuart Kauffman used in his theory to define first-order combinations – molecules colliding to form the building blocks of life. Johnson talks about networks, and more specifically liquid networks that enable a flow of ideas: 'When you work alone in an office, peering into a microscope, your ideas get trapped in place, stuck in your own initial biases. The social flow of the group conversation turns that private solid state into a liquid network.'[14] Johnson's view is that most offices, because of their fixed structures, 'have a natural tendency to disrupt liquid networks'. He suggests that the most inventive places are hives of activity where people get together and share ideas – 'architects and designers are learning how to build work environments that facilitate liquid networks in more permanent structures.'[15]

Deep Work author Cal Newport described architect David Dewane's concept of the Eudaimonia Machine as the ultimate space to achieve the deepest possible work: a single-storey structure of five rooms placed in a line, with no corridor so people are forced to pass through each room to get to the next, means you can't bypass a space as you dive deeper into the machine.

The first room is the gallery, set to inspire. Then the salon with coffee, wi-fi and bar, to create an atmosphere of curiosity.

> Beyond the salon you enter the library. This room stores the permanent record of all work produced in the machine . . . the next room is the office space . . . for 'low-intensity activity'. The final room is a collection of 'deep work chambers' to allow total focus and uninterrupted work flow.[16]

At Stanford Business School, Martin Ruef investigated the relationship between business innovation and diversity. He discovered that the most creative individuals consistently had broad social networks which extended outside their organization and involved people from diverse backgrounds. These diverse, horizontal social networks were more innovative than uniform vertical networks. This research talks to the *scuole* of Venice, which blended people from different backgrounds and professions.

The needs of people have been explored in numerous theories, from Abraham Maslow's famous hierarchy of needs described in his 1943 paper 'A Theory of Human Motivation' to Frederick Herzberg's measures of workplace satisfaction based on hygiene and motivation factors. The idea of 'self-actualization' determined by the need for belonging and recognition that Maslow identified contrasts with the lower-level 'hygiene factors' that Herzberg saw as an influence on dissatisfaction at work – where working environments typically influence how we feel.

A sentient workplace is an interesting way to approach this subject. Hertzberg would look at the workplace from the angle of how satisfied people are. This is influenced by the surroundings as much as the amenities provided in the office. Basic environmental conditions of fresh air, daylight and cleanliness are complemented by the more interesting determinants of the character and personality of a space. Diversity in design can create the variety of aesthetic approaches that resonate with the personal preferences of people. To give an example: providing a space with a mix of different styles of furniture, from modernist to classical, is likely to appeal to more people than providing a narrow, uniform choice of chairs.

Susan Cain's 'kaleidoscope' can be manifested by diversity in colour, noise, lighting, visual privacy, furniture, fabrics and materials. Lighting can be varied through the day, modelling our circadian rhythms and the natural world with its varied landscapes and habitats. And these changes and natural rhythms can be extended to modify experience through a month or a year, as the seasons and cycles of business life (business planning, reviews and events) demarcate different needs at different stages. Diversity is cyclical as well as a constant for the organization.

WITH DIVERSITY COMES inclusion. People need to feel they belong, and if specific needs relating to such issues as mobility or sight impairment are taken into account, a more egalitarian approach can be taken. This is where inclusive design is so important. Rather than treating different needs as 'special needs' – ramps for step-free access, wheelchair-friendly toilets or big-type readable signs, for example – they should be designed seamlessly into the environment we all use for work. Inclusive design helps all of us. It should not be a tick-box exercise for office designers seeking to meet the minimum standards required by discrimination legislation, it should be a celebration of diversity within the organization. As Kay Sargent, director of workplace at architects HOK, told us: 'Diversity is counting the people. Inclusion makes the people count.'[17]

Already we are seeing workplaces provide parent rooms, multifaith spaces, gender-neutral bathrooms and mindfulness zones. These provide places for people based on their specific needs, but they also cater for our changing circumstances as a society. Not every company can afford them, but sleep pods and 'chill-out zones', maker spaces and music rooms, massage and exercise facilities all provide for diversity through the working day and allow people with specific requirements, ranging from baby feeding to workout, jetlag to mental stress, to feel accommodated.

If these environments satisfy the criteria of Maslow and Hertzberg, can we say that space is aligned? It is clear that people can vary their behaviour and personality by choice as well. Just because a Myers–Briggs typology suggests that you are more suited to a specific environment, it doesn't imply that this is the only solution. Sometimes people need to be pushed out of their comfort zone, to have a space that makes them feel uncomfortable or exposes them to different ways of thinking.

'Jelly Bean Working' is one of our own philosophies to celebrate diversity at work. The Jelly Bean is a 'presence' icon which uses technology to alert colleagues anywhere in the world to where you are located and what you are doing. Just as each sweet is distinguished by flavour and colour, so choice and variety are synonymous with the principles of David Dewane's Eudaimonia model: different spaces stimulate different responses and are best suited to different activities or tasks. The rise of the Jelly Bean is analogous to the forces being described that are shifting the gravity towards a new paradigm for the workplace – one that is based on diversity and choice as well as preference and your 'favourite flavour'.

The Jelly Bean focuses on Generation Z, the demographic coming to the workplace next, who have never known a world without the internet and social media, and view technology as an extension of their own minds and bodies. They will inhabit a digital world that is personalized. They consume content based on their preferences and channels, they see their friends and tribes through social media, and they gravitate to places that energize them: where they feel they belong and where they can engage with like-minded people on their terms, both in the physical and digital worlds.

Author Steven Johnson reflects: 'I prefer another metaphor drawn from nature: the reef. What makes the reef so inventive is not the struggle between the organisms but the way they have learned to collaborate – the coral and the zooxanthellae and the parrotfish borrowing and reinventing each other's work.'[18] It is in this biodiversity that we see as the optimal workplace – one that provides Cain's kaleidoscope, Dewane's Eudaimonia Machine and our Jelly Bean approach to celebrate the fact that we are all different and should be accommodated with choice and variety as a core principle.

Rooftop park at Facebook's Menlo Park campus in Palo Alto, California, designed by Frank Gehry, 2018. Staggered seating levels with tropical plants aim to boost health and well-being.

11 Well-Being

Would you be willing to give a sample of your DNA to your employer so that your work environment could be scientifically redesigned to improve your personal health and well-being? This question posed by Tom Savigar of the Future Laboratory at a Worktech conference in 2017 was not a rhetorical one. Nor did it belong to science fiction. Savigar, a leading researcher on lifestyle futures, was simply suggesting that handing over your DNA to an HR department might be 'the next privacy bump' for employees operating like 'everyday athletes' in an always-on 'performance economy'.[1] Savigar was also acknowledging that technology now exists to co-opt office workers into an optimization race whether we like it or not – and whether we are physically in the office or not.

What we eat at work, how often we move around, and even whom we talk to and for how long, will increasingly be scrutinized as companies gather more and more data on each employee every working day through sensors and telemetry inside smart office buildings. Performance targets could include lifestyle goals such as losing weight, as poor individual well-being is seen as a barrier to raising productivity. Sitting at the desk for too long? Always sneaking off to the vending machine for a sugar fix? Never been seen at the salad bar? The bosses of the future will have something to say about that – and they'll have stats to show you too. Imagine your line manager kicking off your appraisal meeting with: 'How are you? In fact, never mind – we already have the graphs.'

Today there are corporate bribes for the better lifestyle – loans to purchase bicycles, train season-ticket advances to kick the car habit, space plans that encourage walking – so we are already heading down that road. But what comes next could significantly remodel the contract between companies and employees, intruding into personal habits and interfering in private well-being to an unprecedented degree. In these shifting privacy boundaries surrounding health at work, there is the inescapable sense of an important frontier about to be breached.

It isn't just the body that will be targeted. A healthier workplace will seek to optimize the mind too. Indeed, the mind market for 'wellness' is growing faster than the body market. This is because organizations and the people who keep them running are more aware today of the mental health implications of trying to balance life and work in the 24/7 digital economy. According to the Global Wellness Institute, workplace well-being has become a burgeoning industry worth just under £40 billion.

Much of the impetus behind the wellness industry has come since the global financial crash of 2008. This resulted in a prolonged exhibition of job insecurity, anxiety and burnout in the workplace that gradually led to investment by both companies and individuals in an increasingly broad array of facilities and services focused on health and well-being. Very quickly, those working inside larger organizations entered a mind- and body-enhancing era of green walls, social staircases, corporate gyms, salad lunches, rooftop gardens, fruit smoothies, cry rooms, safe spaces, walking meetings and office fun runs. It has all become exhausting. As Tom Savigar wryly pointed out: 'Wellness is becoming a tsunami of stress for people.' This view is widely shared. Jim Taylour, Head of Design and Well-Being at furniture maker Orangebox, told us: 'Well-being is just the WD40 for failing processes.'[2]

HOWEVER, IT WAS not always like that; indeed, for most of the last hundred years, it was nothing like that at all. The Quakers who set up those pioneering work-life communities clearly had the paternalistic welfare of their employees in mind – often to keep them from drink. But the modern office of the early twentieth century, rooted in the relentless motion of the machine, was far more interested in the productivity of workers than their well-being. Office work was a stern, unbending system as little concerned with the psychology and mental health of the worker as a turbine is concerned with the sparks that fly when it turns. As office work appeared to involve much less physical effort and danger than working in a factory or a mine, there wasn't much interest in physical safety either. If the issue of employee health arose at all, it was simply as an expedient to keep people in place as cogs in the machine. Sickness and absenteeism were feared and frowned upon.

Even when the more user-friendly contours of the social democratic office were shaped with the involvement of work councils and unions in the 1970s, and personnel departments were renamed Human Resources in a bid to scale up their influence inside organizations, much of management simply chose to ignore that something called well-being existed. Many innovations in modern office design were to impress clients and investors, not for the benefit of the workforce. British and American business leaders in particular continued to view organizations as 'giant pieces of engineering', in Charles Handy's phrase, whose nuts constantly needed to be tightened. Efficiency theory and machine metaphors dominated through a succession of management fads, from business process re-engineering to benchmarking and downsizing.

Even today, there is still some confusion and uncertainty in management circles about what well-being at work really means. Organizations know the costs of poor employee well-being, especially poor mental health. According to a report by Deloitte, the cost of poor mental health among staff increased by 16 per cent between 2017 and 2020, costing companies up to £45 billion across the UK. What they're less clear about is how to devise an effective well-being strategy on a company-wide scale. That is in part because well-being is seen as a personal thing and remains ill-defined in the organizational context, especially when related to collective rather than individual performance.

The situation has been further complicated in the aftermath of the global coronavirus pandemic, which brought public health considerations around safety and social distancing to the heart of the workplace, and brought the effects of remote working and social isolation on mental health to the heart of the workforce. We've all been struck by the devastating impact of successive lockdowns on the ability to work effectively – the exhausting cycle of video calls, the makeshift office on the kitchen table, the endless distractions and, in some cases, digital surveillance by the employer.[3]

When Worktech Academy organized a panel of experts during lockdown to explore the future of workplace well-being, their definitions fell into two main categories: first, a feeling of personal joy, purpose, contentment and thriving; and second, being able to manage challenges and face any problems that arise knowing that support is available. These responses broadly reflected the type of definitions evident in academic research, which tend to conform to a model of personal well-being as subjective and dynamic, and encompassing such things as happiness, job satisfaction, freedom from anxiety and feeling worthwhile. As one of these experts, mental health writer Mark Rice-Oxley, told us: 'COVID-19 has affected the solidity of the architecture of the three well-being elements: financial security, physical health and social connection.'[4]

We have witnessed a rise in loneliness in society, especially post-pandemic. We are social animals, and the workplace has always had a part to play, from purpose and inclusion to networks, friends and relationships. Lockdowns limited social interaction. Hybrid working and the 'new normal' risk exacerbating these trends. Workplace well-being and loneliness are intrinsically linked.

One widely accepted definition that we've found useful is based on research by the New Economics Foundation. It describes well-being as the 'equilibrium' between a person's own psychological, physical and social resources, and external circumstances and challenges. Factors affecting well-being at work include personal resources ('who you are') – your health, activity and work-life balance; and organizational systems ('where you work') – environmental factors, social value of work, technology and infrastructure, social interactions and relationships, and sense of control.[5]

The search for balance between what you bring as an individual and what the workplace or organization offers by way of challenge or support is a helpful model in many ways. It accurately presents well-being as a dynamic state that is constantly oscillating and subject to change, making provision for it a complex affair that cannot be treated as a tick-box exercise. It creates a frame for what companies should think about in terms of office planning and design. And it gives designers something tangible to work with as they try to match the features of the physical workplace to the attributes and needs of the individual. Within this model, giving employees a 'sense of control' is especially important – it features heavily in academic research as an established driver of well-being at work and has wide application.

In the workplace, a 'sense of control' applies to choices regarding work-life balance, surrounding environment, commuting and travel; it also refers to control in terms of access to tools, resources, spaces, control over territory and privacy, and control over relationships and interactions with others in the office community. It extends to personalization of workspace and employee participation into the design process itself, which has been shown to support well-being to some degree.

When British psychologist Craig Knight conducted an experimental study in 2010 to test worker well-being in different environmental conditions, he discovered that giving people the opportunity to arrange their own space with plants and pictures improved their performance in a series of cognitive tests; when that sense of control was removed, productivity immediately reduced and errors increased.[6] A sense of control is not only positive for an individual's well-being, it also helps employees engage with their employer. In 2020, research from Brunel University in the UK led by Mohammad Foroudi found that having more personal control in the workplace has a positive effect on identification with the company.[7]

It doesn't take a detective to work out why a sense of control should be so important at work. Substantial changes to our ways of working have had a dramatic effect on our perceptions of personal control in the workplace. On the one hand, the rise of knowledge working has allowed people to work more autonomously across time and space using technologies that suit them. This increased freedom and choice has given people better insights into how they work best. However, the move away from individually assigned desks to flexible work in an activity-based model has also raised issues around privacy, identity and belonging – and has reduced or damaged well-being for certain groups. For many workers, despite the promise of greater autonomy and choice, new ways of working have signalled a loss of personal control.

In 2018, a report by the Work Foundation at Lancaster University predicted that a rapid rise in flexible working practices might dampen productivity rather than improve it because of a corresponding rise in stress.[8] Amid the sudden acceleration of remote working in the global pandemic that followed two years later, this warning was borne out. There was a well-being 'bounce' in the early months of lockdown, with McKinsey research reporting that 80 per cent of home workers were enjoying the experience. But soon the cracks started to appear.

In the first large-scale survey of opinion conducted in summer 2020 by IBM, which interviewed 3,450 executives in twenty countries, employees complained that they felt tired, overworked, disconnected and unsupported.[9] This was in stark contrast to the views of their bosses who thought things were going well and that they'd done a very good job of rapidly pivoting their organizations to remote working. A subsequent study of 1,200 individuals by the Martec Group recorded a significant decline in mental health, job motivation and job satisfaction among people working from home.[10] Around a third of employees in the survey not only disliked working from home but thought that their company was handling the pandemic badly. Only 16 per cent of those surveyed could be said to be thriving.

Neuroscience has an explanation for such results. Experts suggest that the well-being deficit experienced by workers during the pandemic was due to changes in the brain. People spending all day at home on endless video calls are likely to suffer from deprivation of their neural networks. They are deprived of emotional and behavioural cues, seeing colleagues only through a screen without direct eye contact, and they're deprived of external stimuli that are normally provided by commuting and the random encounters of office life. Without the regular level of electro-chemical 'hits' that the brain craves, people can 'switch off' and experience a dip in energy and creativity. Neuroscientist Dr Fiona Kerr, founder of the Neurotech Institute and an adjunct professor at the University of Adelaide, told us: 'The big challenge for organizations is that the kind of communications that build trust in a team do not travel well through a digital screen, as our neurons are not being fired properly.'[11]

Even without going into the specifics of brain chemistry, it is clear that just as spending long, regimented hours at an office desk is unhealthy, so too is a never-ending stretch on the computer in a spare bedroom or at the kitchen table. At a time of growing job insecurity, many people damaged their own well-being by putting in long hours at home in an attempt to demonstrate that they were indispensable. They refused breaks and risked burnout. As one senior academic told us, 'We used to take work home; now we are living with work at home all the time.' The answer for companies seeking to maintain well-being across an increasingly dispersed workforce is to offer a mixed work diet which combines some face-to-face meeting and social events in the office with the flexibility to work from home as life dictates. This is the 'hybrid' model of working now taking shape in various permutations.

AS WE HAVE seen, today the impact of different work strategies on personal well-being is well documented. But the task of making the link between employee health and company performance is proving much harder to achieve. Research suggests that simple metrics such as sickness, absenteeism or presenteeism alone are not meaningful measures as they don't provide critical information for employers to establish directions at the organizational level. In the absence of any guiding star, companies have busied themselves with various well-being interventions – from company quizzes and virtual cocktails to yoga and mindfulness – aimed at getting people to feel better and work together in order to improve company performance.

In the period between the global financial crash and the coronavirus outbreak, investment in well-being by companies began to flow with two chief characteristics. First, initiatives were mainly reactive (the 'WD40 effect'), based on addressing the negative impacts of poor well-being – sickness, burnout, stress, depression and so on – as opposed to proactively promoting a health-inducing workplace. Second, organizations tended to favour place over people – they prioritized expensive real-estate 'trophy assets' such as 24-hour gyms, healthy food bars and wellness spas over programmes aimed at human communication and support.

Since the pandemic, many employers have come around to the idea that proactive investment in well-being puts the company on the front foot; fixing things when they are already broken – offering therapy to staff, for example – is an uphill struggle, and poor well-being in the organization can be hard to turn around. At the same time, large investments in such office assets as high-end gyms have come under closer scrutiny. Senior leaders are asking: is that what our people *really* need?

The sentient workplace reflects both how you feel and how you measure it. It is the culmination of the attributes that contribute to well-being discussed in this chapter. From nature to nurture, the way we work and the working environment impact our physiology. But, as was put into stark perspective by the pandemic, the workplace also directly determines your physical health. COVID-19 raised the awareness that surfaces can transmit infection, that air quality and ventilation correlate with viral transmission, and that density and proximity impact contagion.

Employees returning to offices after long lockdowns will expect to know and see the quality of the environment. They will prefer to touch fewer items in the office environment, so new technologies such as voice control will become more prevalent in the workplace. Measuring humidity, pollutants or volatile organic compounds (vocs) and CO_2 levels, and displaying the results on digital dashboards in the office space, will demonstrate how seriously employers take well-being.

In the future, we are likely to see the idea of workplace well-being as a balance between personal resources ('who you are') and organizational systems ('where you work') play out in a world of work far removed from the Taylorist clerks who punched the clock or the social democrats empowered to stroll down faux corporate boulevards. The office will not be the main container for work, so it will not be the main container for well-being. But as part of a more flexible mix, it will continue to play a critical role in building culture, teamwork and morale. Within the walls of the office, a sense of control, which was once so prized by the management hierarchy, will finally belong to the workforce. Allowing people to shift furniture around, decorate their own spaces, manage local ambient and environmental conditions, or engage in co-creation practices aimed at giving them a voice in how their workspace is designed, are ways to achieve an equilibrium always denied in the past.

12 Hybridity

Long before the concept of hybrid working captured the public imagination during the global pandemic, there was already a growing conversation around hybridity in working life. This took many forms. At its most basic, 'hybrid' means mixture, and different elements are now being mixed together to reassemble work and workplace with a new set of combinations. Researchers in the social sciences, arts and humanities have used the term 'hybridity' to describe the ways in which discrete social practices or structures combine to generate new social practices or structures. So, what are the main themes of the hybrid office? What is being mixed together, and why? We have discovered that hybridity takes many forms and comes in varying doses.

Historically, the modern office was pure in concept and singular in development. It stood apart from the rest of the city, aloof even from the local neighbourhood or district. Its forbidding facades revealed little of what went on inside and its connections with the world outside were weak. Its doors were closed and access was guarded. Entry was privileged and, once inside the belly of the beast, people were required to leave their personal lives behind and submit to a system that demanded

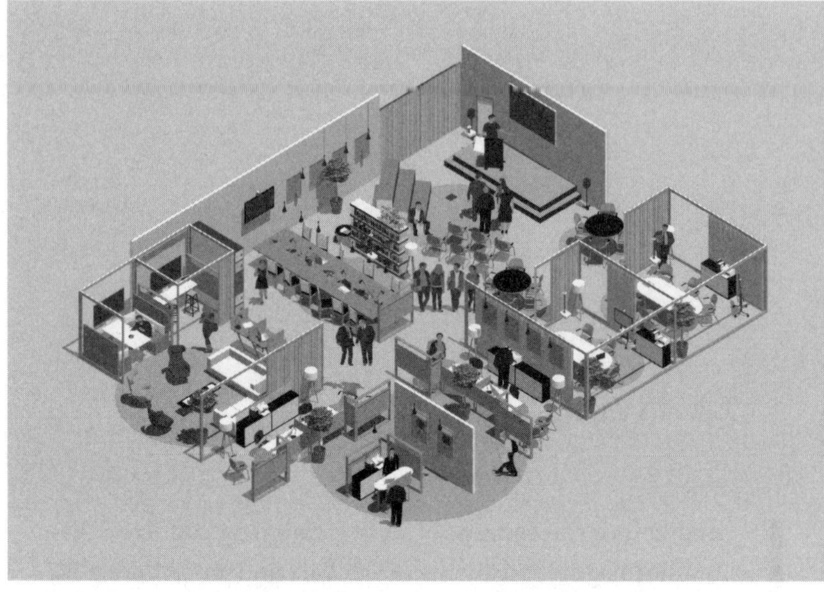

Hybrid concept for UniCredit bank branch, 2016. The bank shares half of its space with other services such as coworking and an entrepreneur club. Designed by Andrew Thompson, Royal College of Art.

total commitment to a single organizational purpose for a set number of hours. The endurance of the modern office for more than a hundred years was due in no small part to its single-minded character. Today, a key dimension of the reinvention of the office is that it is becoming a hybrid and permeable environment, not a singular and opaque one.

Office buildings once stood by themselves in central business districts or suburban science parks; now workspace is being woven into the urban fabric, taking its place as part of an 'intermix' of retail, residential, transport, educational and cultural functions. Brick-and-mortar offices that once commanded our daily presence must now share our attention with the bits and bytes of virtual work, as nodes in an increasingly fluid network.

Within workspace itself, we are seeing the homogenous provision of routine work settings disrupted by the appearance of cafés, bookshops, maker spaces, galleries, coworking lounges and other amenities, which are set to reanimate the office with a broader range of uses. The permanent infrastructure of the workplace is being complemented by temporary or transient infrastructures, drawn from adjacent worlds of theatre, exhibition and hospitality design. The office is even preparing for the most radical combo of all – a world of augmented work in which people share the same workplace with robots and other forms of machine intelligence.

ONE OF THE most far-reaching examples of hybridity in the world of work is the emergence in city planning of the 'smart urban precinct'. These digital districts, as they're also called, are 'built from the internet up'; their workplaces are nestled in alongside other urban functions as opposed to being separated from them, and they comprise a mix of physical and digital space. These are innovation districts, and they build on prior experience in designing for creative clusters and mixed-use developments. However, they go a stage further in the way they integrate physical experiences with data-driven services and smart technologies.

We coined the term 'intermix' to describe the essential characteristics of these smart precincts.[1] Examples can be found at King's Cross in London, at Australia Technology Park (ATP) in Sydney and at Songdo, close to Seoul. Some smart precincts are led by flexible workspace, as in the case of ATP; others are built around a large retail cluster or a residential offer or a transport hub, as in the case of the King's Cross regeneration project in London.

We came up with terms to describe these different conditions: Emporium, featuring a bustling shopping centre as the central element; Haven, which has a smart home quarter at its core;

Interchange, where a transport hub takes centre stage; and Enterprise, a workspace-led district. We also found new districts being built around an anchor tenant that is a major employer locally, such as Port Covington in Baltimore, designed to accommodate the large sporting goods brand Under Armour, or themed around health care and education, such as a new 2,800-hectare (7,000 ac) mixed-use development at Lake Nona in Orlando.

Carefully curated hybrid precincts of this type aim to be a destination at all times, not a business district that is totally dead in the evenings and at weekends. They don't just mix building uses or the physical and the digital either. They encourage public–private partnerships, co-locate start-ups next to large corporates and small specialist stores next to major retail chains, and generally try to blend work and life in a way that strictly zoned cities, which cordoned off office districts for decades, have failed to do in the past. In some ways, these precincts represent a twenty-first-century bid to recreate the kind of vibrant, mixed-use urban

The Google groundscraper at King's Cross, London, designed by Heatherwick Studio and Bjarke Ingels Group (BIG), 2018. This office building is a central element of the mixed-use King's Cross innovation district.

communities that were a feature of large cities before urban planners destroyed them with new expressways and underpasses (think of what planner Robert Moses did to Manhattan in the 1930s). But they're not always welcomed by local communities.

In 2017, the City of Toronto announced a partnership with Sidewalk Labs, the urban tech subsidiary of Google parent company Alphabet, to develop Quayside, a 5-hectare (12 ac) slice of Toronto's east waterfront. This smart precinct would be a test bed for new ideas and catalyse a local tech-led economy. Plans included snow-melting sidewalks and automated awnings to mitigate the harsh Canadian winters. Walkable streets, autonomous vehicles, modular wooden towers, eco-friendly building materials and garbagebots were also part of a sustainable package of proposals submitted for public consultation. But things quickly came unstuck amid citizen mistrust over where data generated by the project would be stored. Within three years, the project collapsed as Sidewalk Labs unceremoniously pulled out.

Despite this high-profile setback, however, we predict that digital districts are set to be a growing part of the landscape of work. The presence of Google at King's Cross or Boston Consulting Group, WarnerMedia and Wells Fargo in Hudson Yards is testament to their pulling power. But companies today are not just eyeing up relocating to more vibrant, mixed-use districts, they are looking at ways to leverage redundant space in their existing real-estate portfolios by finding new ways to share overheads, generate revenue and draw more people into the space.

This is a particular issue for the big banks who have vast branch networks lying idle as more of us bank online. The economic case for keeping large single-use bank branches open makes little sense given reduced footfall, but banks also want to maintain a foothold with local communities. In 2016, we began working with the Italian banking and financial services company UniCredit on a research project to make better use of its large and echoing banking halls. UniCredit wanted to get closer to the communities it serves and create a better environment for its employees while reducing real-estate costs.

The joint study was called 'Hybrid Space Making', and our hypothesis was that banking services could be combined with other customer-facing facilities such as bookshops, cafés, restaurants or coworking spaces, thus spreading the cost of maintaining a branch network.[2] We also wanted these hybrid retail banking spaces to mix digital services into physical location. With hindsight, the project appeared ahead of its time. The research team searched for hybrid precedents in London and Milan, and mapped their characteristics; co-creation workshops were held with UniCredit employees and customers to define user needs.

The project went on to develop an architectural 'kit of parts' to flexibly repurpose the bank's branches for more hybrid uses. A service bar – common to retail, hospitality, work and banking spaces – was identified as the main activation device for each space, as part of a modular design approach. Digital services to enhance the interactions between people and place were then layered onto our blueprint. The project created three models for the future hybrid bank branch, each at a different scale, from mini-hybrid (90 per cent of the space given to banking) through midi-hybrid (50 per cent of the space) to maxi-hybrid (only 10 per cent). New partnerships and joint ventures with a range of commercial operators were envisaged as part of the strategy.

In July 2017, UniCredit converted a former traditional bank branch in Via Verdi, Milan, into a mini-hybrid business centre, combining coworking, meeting and event spaces. Klaus Sandbiller, UniCredit's head of Global Real Estate Projects, told the *Corporate Real Estate Journal*:

> Additional social value can be created by opening space to the community, providing a physical platform for

> interaction and collaboration in the digital world. The principle of using space more efficiently, and to share it with other services in combination with increased user experience, will lead to new models of property management and intermediation.[3]

SIMILAR IDEAS AROUND providing social value and a platform for interaction can be seen in another theme of hybridity – the effect on permanent, rigid and inflexible infrastructures of the office by the introduction of more temporary or permeable structures and practices. Techniques drawn from retail, hotel and exhibition design have been evident in making the workplace more 'clubbable' for some time, and this trend will only accelerate as offices seek to become more attractive as destinations for workers with the choice to work remotely.

However, the world of theatre design is also set to have a growing effect on hybrid workspace. Why? The way offices are currently constructed makes it hard to generate mood and atmosphere in the workplace, unless companies are willing to spend a fortune on fabricating highly customized one-off interiors. A study led by Imogen Privett while at the Helen Hamlyn Centre for Design, Royal College of Art, London, revealed that simple, lightweight and inexpensive stage techniques related to manipulating light, shadow, projection, screens, levels, colour and vista offered the potential to transform the experience of the office with minimum means.[4]

Privett defined a vocabulary of stage elements for application by designers, and the project went on to demonstrate the approach by developing a new office product for manufacture: an illuminated screen system, capable of hanging from a suspended ceiling, to support private concentration and informal collaboration in the open-plan office. This innovation used the same principles as a theatre set being 'flown in' from above. Privett's aim was to bring an 'emotional richness' to the office by emulating the way theatre designers use scale, depth and framing to make spaces and settings more visually arresting. And she took her research further by analysing the design of temporary urban events, such as markets, festivals and pop-ups, to find ways to make offices more dynamic, more spontaneous and less predictable. As with UniCredit's pioneering hybrid placemaking project, Privett's work signalled a direction towards a more mixed and sociable landscape of work.[5]

Perhaps the most telling scenario for hybridity around the future of the workplace is the one in which humans and robots share the same office space. In recent years, much media coverage and large chunks of the internet have been devoted to an

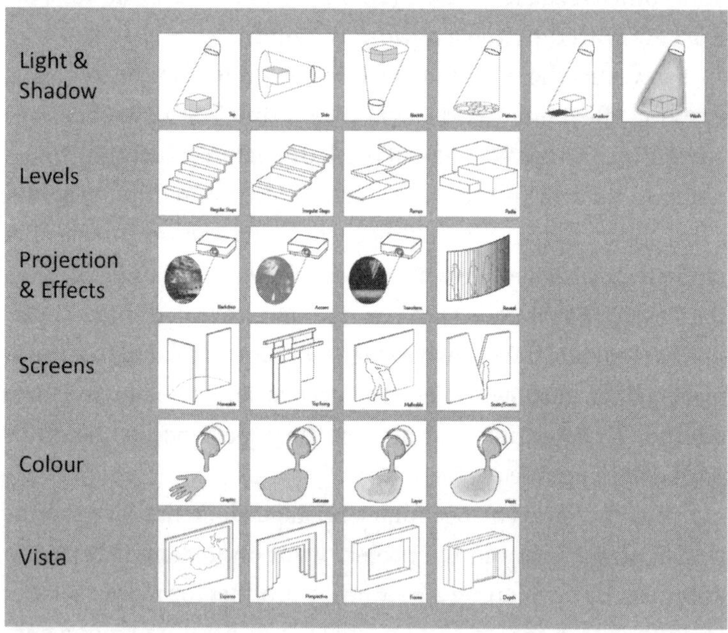

Vocabulary of theatre elements, 2012, designed by Royal College of Art researcher Imogen Privett as a kit of parts to be applied in offices to create more interest and variety.

increasingly hysterical debate about how automation and AI are set to take our jobs. A 2017 *New Yorker* cover by R. Kikuo Johnson, for example, portrayed a dystopian street scene in which robots trundle past a homeless human begging at their feet, and one deigns to lower its gaze to flip a few coins in his cup. As designer and futurist Kevin McCullagh has explained: 'The most widely held fear, and one that taps into our earliest fears about industrialisation, is of mass unemployment as robots take most of the jobs.'[6]

However, as McCullagh also acknowledged, critiques of the proliferation of increased automation and artificial intelligence are now more nuanced; in his view, there is growing acceptance that technological revolutions tend to create more jobs than they destroy, robots often free up humans to do more skilled work, and anyway we have a history of overestimating what machines can do. Fear and panic about losing human jobs to robots is therefore beginning to give way to a growing realization that rather than whole jobs being at risk, individual component tasks of jobs are more likely to be automated. This opens up a more positive scenario in which people and machines work together rather than separately to accomplish things more effectively.

This is the hybrid world of 'augmented work' and, while it brims with new possibilities, it also asks new questions of the workplace. What are the different ways in which robots can augment the work of office employees? And how should workplace design adapt to accommodate the introduction of machine intelligence? When Worktech Academy studied this field and published a report on augmented work, we built on the pioneering work of Kevin McCullagh, referencing a range of five models for human-machine relationships in an ascending scale of robot autonomy.[7] The 'assigned' and 'supervised' models are where machines complete tasks that require significant human input; the 'coexistent' and 'assistive' models shift the balance towards the independence of the machine; the 'symbiotic' model, still some way into the future, is where machines require minimal human input to complete high-level tasks.

The more one considers machine autonomy in augmenting work, the greater the implications for workplace design. One can foresee office buildings with robotic service tunnels, in much the same way that utility tunnels run through many buildings today. Robots will not only benefit from having their own space, humans will too. Robot access tunnels can be small, much smaller than a human would need; they can also be designed without the light, heat or air conditioning, for example, that people need. Eventually, these areas will even incorporate charging and maintenance areas so that robots can remain hidden as much as possible.

Robot-centric design is already beginning to happen. During the pandemic, extensive use was made of robot security guards and robot cleaners. Further developments like automated drone ports at the top of buildings show robots making use of spaces that could never be accessed by humans. At the Mansueto Library at the University of Chicago, the entire 3.5-million book collection is housed in high-density racking in 15-metre-high (50 ft) shelves. It is managed by a robotic retrieval and delivery system in a 743-square-metre (8,000 sq. ft) underground complex. This area is designed exclusively for the robotic system to work in and cannot be used by humans.

In the life science industry, workplace strategists are already thinking about a scenario in which machines and scientists will share the same space, bringing a new level of efficiency and creativity to labs. Such lab space might be redesigned so that researchers, freed from supervising routine experiments, are given natural daylight and better vistas on the perimeter of the facility to think imaginatively, while the heavy machinery hums away in the middle of deep floor plates and in basements.

In general, it's true that we're already sharing the workplace with a ton of machine intelligence – just think about digital ceilings, pervasive wi-fi, generative office design using algorithms or smart building systems with predictive analytics. The hybrid workspaces of the future will find a place not just for people to collaborate, but for humans and machines too.

Intergenerational interaction as part of a Panasonic research project with the Helen Hamlyn Centre for Design, Royal College of Art, 2013. The study looked at the use of digital technology to support older people.

13 Demography

The reinvention of the modern office is unfolding against the backdrop of the changing demographic make-up of the workforce. Behind the adaptation of the places and spaces, systems and structures, ideologies and identities that we've explored in this book are the people who will occupy tomorrow's workplace. The mid-twentieth-century office population – 'the family-formation workforce' of 21- to 45-year-olds, as economists have described it – was overwhelmingly white, able-bodied and male. Today, if you walk into any large office space, you are likely to encounter four different generations at work. Legislation addressing age and disability discrimination in the workplace has removed some of the barriers to people of different abilities; women have broken through the glass ceiling in some previously male-dominated companies; and there is now more awareness and discussion of the obstacles that have faced people of colour.

So, as we discussed earlier, there is today a less homogenous workforce in search of a less homogenous workplace. If we look at demographic groups, the lion's share of the attention by employers has inevitably been on the newer entrants to workforce – Millennials (b. 1980–94) and Generation Z (b. 1995–2012) – as they represent the future and their status as 'digital natives' and 'digital dependants' align them most closely with new ways of working. Three out of four people in the workplace will be Millennials by 2025, according to some projections, and this generational cohort is at the epicentre of what is charmlessly described as 'the war for talent', as organizations jostle to recruit and retain the best people. We shouldn't underestimate the influence of Millennials in driving change in the office and promoting a move towards more autonomous, flexible work styles over the past decade or so.

Gen Z already make up a quarter of the global workforce and command attention because of their special and unprecedented relationship with technology. Many of these brand-new entrants were hired, onboarded and inducted during the pandemic without setting foot in the workplace or meeting their employer face-to-face. Today, they continue to work remotely on projects with colleagues they have never met, conducting the whole business over video. Many observers suggest that the attitudes and preferences of Gen Z will shape the future of the workplace more decisively than any other cohort before it. According to a study by the Workforce Institute, a think tank, Gen Z is a contradictory cohort: they won't tolerate being forced to work when they don't want to, but they also consider themselves to be the hardest-working generation in the workforce, as they grew up watching their parents and friends lose their jobs and homes after the great financial crash.[1]

Generation Z is often seen as an extension of the Millennial generation, but the two generations differ in terms of behaviour and outlook. Gen Z workers have never known a world without the internet and social media – they are digital dependants. Technology informs every aspect of their lives, from boxset streaming and online gaming to social media and monitoring global news.

They are most comfortable with visual media – video technology is important to them. Millennials, on the other hand, spend more time behind a desktop and keyboard set-up than on their phones, according to research.[2] Email and instant messaging is their first port of call before video-calling another colleague.

Before the pandemic, organizations were beginning to adapt and transform their workspaces towards agile working practices to accommodate Millennial expectations. Today there is growing focus on video-centric trends that accelerated during the COVID-19 periods of lockdown and appeal to the Gen Z outlook. The challenge for employers is to provide a better all-round digital experience than the one their new Gen Z recruits managed at home during the pandemic. This task will require a workplace that is much lighter on its feet and more serious about connectivity.

The differences between the two groups of digital natives don't stop at technology: when it comes to the environment and sustainability as an issue in the workplace, studies suggest that Gen Z employees are less passive than their Millennial predecessors. They want to see practical action on climate change and are not mollified by corporate statements of intent or high-minded policy declarations by employers. Only real efforts by companies to reduce their carbon footprint as responsible global citizens will meet Gen Z expectations. This will have a knock-on effect on where office buildings are located and how they are built and run. It explains a growing interest by large companies in the circular economy, which emphasizes better use of resources through reuse, recycling and redesign.

AT THE OTHER end of the demographic spectrum, we find the Baby Boomers (b. 1946–64) still very much in the game. More than 40 million of them can be found still at work in the American economy. The U.S. Bureau of Labor Statistics projects that a quarter of the country's labour force will be 55 or over by 2024. That is up from 22 per cent in 2014 and just 12 per cent in 1994. In Britain, meanwhile, the number of over-seventies in full or part-time employment has more than doubled to around half a million since 2009. The USA actually has a higher rate of employment for people aged 65 to 69 than Britain or Germany, although as many as two-thirds of workers say they have seen or experienced age discrimination in the U.S. workplace.

Stigma and stereotyping still persists around a perceived weakening of productivity among older workers, although there is considerable evidence to the contrary and attitudes are changing. Research in 2016 from the Milken Institute's Center for the Future of Aging and the Stanford Center on Longevity found that older employees took fewer sick days, showed stronger problem-solving skills and were more likely to be highly satisfied at work than younger colleagues.[3] Neither are older workers Luddites when it comes to new technologies: a study by two economists, MIT's Daron Acemoglu and Boston University's Pascual Restrepo, revealed that U.S. metropolitan areas that have gone through faster population ageing have also adopted technologies with greater automation.[4]

When two London Business School professors, Lynda Gratton and Andrew J. Scott, published *The 100-Year Life: Living and Working in the Age of Longevity* in 2016, their thesis crystallized how our ability to live longer lives will transform the world of work. Gratton and Scott argued that we need to abandon the traditional, linear three-stage life progression comprised of education, career and then retirement, and replace it with a multiple-phased life course where people keep learning throughout their lives, take lots of breaks, and dip in and out of jobs and careers.[5] Hiring of workers should be based on age-neutral metrics such as skills rather than narrowly defined academic credentials, which tend to be more important if you're taking on people straight from university.

In 2020, at the start of the global pandemic, Gratton and Scott followed up with a second volume, *The New Long Life: A Framework for Flourishing in a Changing World*. This sketches out the considerable institutional changes that will be needed to underpin an age of longevity, when people no longer retire from the office in the way they once did. Gratton and Scott call on all of us to become 'social pioneers' in making those societal changes happen.[6]

They also argue for a culture of greater flexibility – not just more working from home, which was already happening, but other ideas too. Their suggestions range from a four-day working work to the replacement of mandatory retirement ages with optional retirement paths, thus breaking down the linear, monolithic construct of office life still further. They anticipate that rapid technological change could lead to more, rather than less, training for older workers as digital learning could be delivered at scale. Lynda Gratton told us that 'COVID-19 represents a massive break in the history of work which is opening the door to an age of experiment. Companies need to be flexible with time as well as space.'[7]

Some companies, such as Boeing, have already done away with a fixed retirement age, and workers can continue to be gainfully employed into their 'old age'. Boeing's longest-serving employee, Diana Rhea, started in 1942 as a twenty-year-old clerk and retired in 2017 at the age of 95. Clearly, demographic pressures are exerting an unseen influence on how work and workplace is being reshaped.

Sandwiched between the older workers and the newbies, we find Generation X employees (b. 1965–79), who are increasingly occupying positions of seniority in the workforce but receive far less attention than other generations. Worried about work-life balance, moving easily between jobs and preferring a casual work environment, Gen X workers are in danger of being the forgotten generation – or ending up 'burnt-out, bottlenecked and bored', to borrow a memorable phrase used by researchers Robert Morison, Tamara Erickson and Ken Dychtwald in the *Harvard Business Review* to describe a workplace affliction called 'middlescence'.[8] Their predicament was summed up by writer Rich Cohen: 'Caught between vast, self-regarding waves of boomers and millennials, Generation X is steeped in irony, detachment, and a sense of dread.'[9]

GENERATION X IS nominally part of the 'war for talent' that big employers like to focus on, but efforts to 'attract and retain' are more generally aimed at Millennials and, soon, Gen Z. It is instructive to see how large organizations are making themselves more attractive to the talent pool. When American amenities giant Aramark conducted a survey of practice in the field, its researchers found that the most successful employers were those who invested heavily in workplace experience.[10] At the core of its report was an analysis of companies – many of them from technology, consulting, professional services, retail and hospitality – which appeared in the 'Top 10 Places to Work 2019' listings from LinkedIn, Glassdoor and *Fortune* magazine. Their strategies revolved around a few common themes, including comfort and relaxation; health and well-being, with diet, exercise and mental health support prioritized; fostering social communities with a sense of belonging; purpose and identity; customized food and drink; bringing the outdoors in; and diversity as a source of organizational pride.

These things are not just on the Millennial wish list – they are welcomed by office workers right across the demographic span. Indeed, it can be argued that what the different generations hold in common is far greater than what differentiates them from each other. The pandemic revealed a generational divide between younger workers who wanted to get back to the office and socialize, and older employees happy to stay at home – but this probably had more to do with the respective size of homes occupied by people early in their career and those who had worked long enough to buy a bigger pad.

When the Royal College of Art's Helen Hamlyn Centre for Design conducted a study called Welcoming Workplace in 2009 to explore how companies could stop a 'brain drain' and retain experienced knowledge workers by redesigning the environment, the provision of biophilic spaces for contemplation and retreat was identified as making a difference.[11] However, the research team also discovered that it wasn't just older workers who needed an escape from the desk: all ages felt burnt out and in need of a soothing break during the working day.

The Welcoming Workplace study remains relevant more than a decade later, offering a valuable lesson about the need for inclusive design, or design for all, in the workplace. Raising standards for everyone is what matters, whether that is in the quality of the space provided or in the connectivity of the technology. When the effects of COVID-19 pressed the reset button in the workplace, it wasn't just older workers celebrating a retreat from high-density open-plan space, which has been around since the late 1990s. Dissatisfaction with the noise, distractions and a lack of privacy in the open-plan offices extends to all age groups.

The big squeeze on office real estate over the past twenty years – cramming more people into less space – was sold as necessary to improve collaboration and communication. But a number of scientific studies have challenged this thinking. Harvard researchers Ethan Bernstein and Stephen Turban, for example, looked at communication patterns of employees inside two large organizations making the shift from cubicles to open plan. They found that the level of face-to-face interaction fell by around 70 per cent in both organizations, with a corresponding increase in emailing and instant messaging.[12]

Today, companies must tread more carefully around open office space, whether in relation to social distancing or the wider cultural changes catalysed by the pandemic. Employers should also build a culture that can be relevant right across the age range. The role of play at work is an interesting sidebar in relation to this search for inclusivity. Management fads such as Lego Serious Play, which was lampooned by journalist Dan Lyons in his book *Lab Rats* (2018),[13] have been complemented by a trend towards filling the office with brightly coloured toys – slides, ping-pong tables, artificial beach huts, fish tanks, flying pods with propellers – to engage employees. But should offices be playgrounds for adults? Or as Dan Lyons asked: 'Why has the workplace become a cross between a kindergarten and a Scientology assessment center? . . . Why does work involve such infantilization?'[14]

Google has in the past been particularly associated with this trend to paint in primary colours and treat office workers as small children. When the Foster-designed Apple Park opened in California, the influential critic Lucy Kellaway of the *Financial Times* commended Apple for 'turning its back on fun and going for beauty instead' in its new landmark scheme. Kellaway remarked: 'Apple Park is made for grown-ups. For the past two decades office spaces have been built as if for primary school children . . . This pernicious trend – ugly, stupid and ageist – started in Silicon Valley and has spread.'[15]

Google today is no longer a 'world leader in infantilising its workforce', as Kellaway once accused it of being. In common with its many emulators, it has adopted a more sober approach, the fun and frivolous elements in its offices balanced with cookery classes and other learning opportunities as part of a broad strategy to build cultural capital. Google's own workforce has grown older and it now shares with many other companies the challenge of building a workplace that appeals across the demographic divide. As new labour market entrants ramp up their digital demands and the older workers refuse to go quietly, that challenge will only become harder.

PART III
REINVENTION

Expansive client interaction space in the London headquarters of McKinsey & Company, designed by MoreySmith, 2020. An artful approach to rethinking the stuffy professional services firm.

14 Repurposing

Before the COVID-19 pandemic struck in spring 2020, the reimagining of the modern office was already taking shape, stealthily and almost imperceptibly, without fanfare. The process of reinvention was largely behind closed doors in the hands of workplace professionals – the architects, strategy consultants, real-estate advisors and developers who were quietly and carefully experimenting with new agile space formats and mobile technologies. The leaders of major corporations by and large still clung to the traditional office model, however, and flexible or remote working was not often officially sanctioned by boardrooms.

The impact of COVID-19 brought everything out into the open. With a suddenness that took everyone by surprise, remote working accelerated overnight and questions around the future of work were immediately transported from the arcane margins of professional life to the heart of the popular debate. Would people ever go back to their offices? What would become of our empty business districts? Could we really be productive working from home over a long period? Serious broadsheets devoted countless op-ed articles to the destiny or demise of the office;

television and radio programmes probed the issue; social media lit up with various arguments.

Inside company boardrooms, senior leaders who had previously delegated matters of workplace planning and design to lower orders in the organization now focused on repurposing the office property portfolio with unprecedented attention. As one head of real-estate projects at a large European bank told us: 'Before the pandemic, I used to have an annual meeting with my CEO. I'd put on a suit, visit the executive enclave, work through a formal agenda, go away again. Now I'm on video calls with my CEO every week as we try to figure out the future.' What company leaders chiefly wanted to know was how much office space they were likely to require to run their business in the aftermath of the coronavirus crisis, and what their employees were likely to need in terms of design and amenities to come back to the workplace. These questions were not easy to answer.

As a maelstrom of change swirled around the future of the office with each new announcement by a big employer or government body or trades union or professional association on what could or should happen next, the general picture became harder to discern. Gradually, however, we began to see some clear patterns beginning to emerge in the behaviour of different organizations. Essentially, two rival camps have formed in the aftermath of COVID-19.

In one corner is a group we have named 'resolute returners' – these are companies that unapologetically want everyone permanently back in the office as if the pandemic never happened. They are sceptical about the value of remote working and believe that higher-value interpersonal activities such as innovation, training and mentoring can only be done face to face. However, while promoting the physical workplace as the key to making their business flourish, they also recognize that it will need replanning and redesigning to some extent to be acceptable to returning employees.

In the other corner we have 'choice champions' – these are organizations that are embracing the possibilities of change by adopting a work-from-anywhere model and making flexibility and choice the cornerstone of their new workplace strategy. They recognize that the post-pandemic workplace is not about a simple binary choice between two work channels, home and office. It is about developing a more complex set of flexible options to help the organization perform, essentially creating multiple channels for working. Between these two polar opposites we found a spectrum of different approaches by companies large and small.

'RESOLUTE RETURNERS' HAVE been characterized as Luddites who are simply resisting technological progress. However, they insist their approach is based on an honest appraisal of how critical employee co-location is to building a culture of learning. The loss of an 'over-the-shoulder' training and mentoring aspect has been a major concern during the pandemic, especially in financial and law firms. David Solomon, CEO of Goldman Sachs, has led the charge – he described the remote-work model as an 'aberration' that needs to be corrected as quickly as possible.[1] Citigroup CEO Jane Fraser told the *Financial Times* that 'everyone will return to the office eventually. I think from a cultural point of view – apprenticeship, the sense of belonging – you are better together.'[2] Jamie Dimon, CEO of JPMorgan Chase, also questioned the plausibility of remote working. 'How do you build a culture and character? How are you going to learn properly?' he asked. According to Dimon, 'A lot of work takes place not at the meeting, but before or after the meeting, when people share ideas.'[3]

'Resolute returners' can point to a wealth of employee surveys which reveal that, after an initial honeymoon period with remote working, people began to struggle with working at home and craved a return to the office. A Microsoft trend survey described this process as 'digital exhaustion' as employees began to work longer and longer hours at home without a regular commute to give the day boundaries.[4] However, the same employee surveys also suggest that any return to the office should not involve a return to the pre-COVID-19 status quo of noisy, high-density open-plan spaces. These are now deemed unsafe.

It is clear that offices for returners will need to be redesigned with more enclosures and privacy. Over time, the social distancing workarounds we saw at the start of the global pandemic with one-way systems and rudimentary desk spacing will need to be replaced by genuinely health-inducing office design – the more so as there could be a trust issue among employees compelled by their bosses to return to the workplace. Many firms are today busy upgrading their spaces and systems to make people feel safer and more valued.

'Choice champions' adopting a work-from-anywhere model face different organizational challenges. In trusting their employees to make the right choices over where and how they work, these firms must adapt their leadership models to support this shift and adopt a more customer-centric approach to employee experience and engagement. Choice-led companies will see the rise of what has been described as 'omni-channel workers' in their ranks, using a combination of mobile devices and cloud-based technologies to plug into their work from any location or setting they feel is most productive for them.

Who are these 'choice champions'? Swedish music-streaming platform Spotify, for example, has adopted a model that will allow its 6,550 employees to choose whether they want to be in the office full time, at home full time or use a combination of different channels to conduct their work. Spotify is also redesigning its office space to accommodate employee preferences for quiet spaces, shared-desk space and collaboration areas. U.S. software company Salesforce has offered its employees three options for how they'll work going forward: flex, fully remote and office-based. The flex option will allow workers to come into the office up to three times a week for tasks that cannot be conducted virtually. Salesforce president Brent Hyder commented: 'An immersive workspace is no longer limited to a desk in our towers; the 9-to-5 workday is dead; and the employee experience is about more than ping-pong tables and snacks.'[5]

Business communications platform Slack is giving employees more freedom to choose their working hours and introducing a permanent flexible working policy for the majority of its 1,600-plus employees. Social media giant Twitter has said all its employees can work from home 'forever' if they wish to. Twitter's shift to a permanent remote work policy was already in existence and was accelerated by the pandemic. In 2018, CEO Jack Dorsey sent an email to his employees encouraging them to work from home after experiencing a lift in productivity by doing so himself.

Some observers have made a parallel between 'omni-channel working' and omni-channel retailing or commerce, which provides a single, seamless customer experience across all channels whether you visit a store, shop online or do click-and-collect. Our own research suggests that the coming era of omni-channel working championed by choice-led companies will mean the office building portfolio is used in different ways.[6] Our forecast is that the office will remain a critical channel of work but will evolve within a broader ecosystem of several work channels. The diagram shown on the next page maps out the main work channels, which are sized according to their likely importance.

A 'destination office' will be the place to go to create culture, build social capital and connect to the mission and values of the organization; a 'training office' will provide a dedicated learning

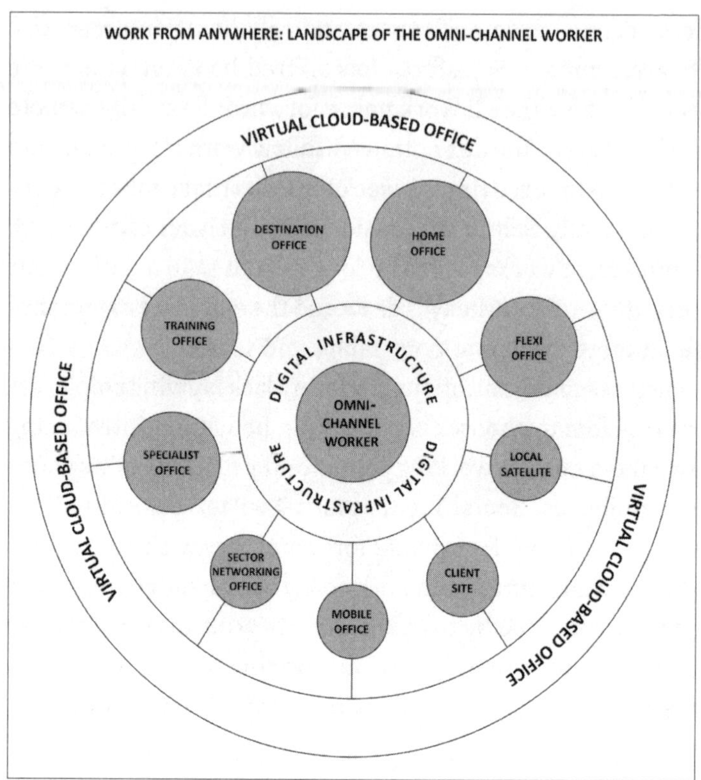

Work from anywhere: the emerging landscape of the 'omni-channel worker'. Worktech Academy/Mirvac (2020).

and mentoring environment; a 'specialist office' will accommodate production and R&D activities with the requirement for regular attendance, such as life science lab facilities or 24-hour media newsrooms; the 'home office' channel will play a more prominent and more permanent role in working life than before the pandemic, but the omni-channel worker will have other options too.

The 'flexi-office' will provide membership of coworking spaces and other space-as-a-service provisions across the city. Local 'satellite' offices will be located closer to people's homes in a hub-and-spoke model that reduces commuting times; and companies will also experiment with mobile offices that offer local convenience. Working at client sites will become more prevalent, as will working at sector-specific clubs and associations – twenty-first-century guilds where the omni-channel worker can network with others in their industry or profession.

WHILE THE 'RESOLUTE returners' and 'choice champions' captured most attention, other groups started to emerge as the global pandemic dragged on. There was a type of organization we identified as 'space shavers' determined not to waste a good crisis – these companies viewed the COVID-19 reset as a once-in-a-lifetime opportunity to reshape and rationalize their real-estate portfolio. In many cases, their main impulse was to reduce the footprint and cut property costs, a long-time corporate preoccupation, although some 'space shavers' also sought to create more flexible and dynamic team-based environments for their people.

One of Britain's biggest regional newspaper publishers, Reach, announced plans to close all but fifteen of its offices in the UK – leaving most of its regional titles without bases in the areas they serve. Reach told most of its journalists they will work permanently from home in future, prompting office closures across the country. It intends to maintain hub offices filled with meeting rooms in key cities such as Belfast, Birmingham, Leeds and Manchester. There was a similar story at Lloyds Banking Group, which made plans to cut its space by 20 per cent after 77 per cent of its 68,000 employees said they wanted to work from home for three or more days a week in the future. William Chalmers, the bank's chief financial officer, said Lloyds would make sure its offices offered more space for teamwork rather than areas where staff sit at solitary desks.[7]

HSBC took space-shaving even further, announcing that it would abandon 40 per cent of its offices in London and other cities around the world but keep its headquarters in Canary Wharf. BP unveiled a new hybrid model, entitled BP Work-Life, to offer employees a more 'flexible, engaging and dynamic' way of working with 40 per cent of their time at home. Across the corporate landscape, big organizations eyed up the opportunities to trim space and repurpose it with fewer desks and more meeting facilities.

The picture was not all about downsizing and rationalization, however. We also noticed a growing group of companies making major investments in new technology, placing their chips on a hybrid model in which augmented reality (AR), virtual reality (VR) and extended reality (XR) – an umbrella term for this type of technology – would assume growing importance. Bank of America, for example, partnered with the start-up Strivr to bring VR into its workplace training; professional service giant PwC announced plans to spend £75 million to redesign many of its offices with café-style meeting areas and equip staff with thousands of VR headsets; Fidelity International executives experimented with a VR auditorium, taking questions from colleagues and walking up and down aisles in a virtual environment; and Swiss bank UBS issued its London-based traders with smart glasses, which it says allows staff to recreate the trading floor experience at home.

The purpose of big tech investment, however, is not just to transform employee experience and engagement in a blended world of physical and digital work, but to capture data and use it to make informed decisions about all aspects of business. We saw how companies were starting to ramp up their data analytics capabilities to better ride out the pandemic, making adjustments to their workplace based on real-time evidence. Scotiabank's W4 ecosystems project is a good example of a data-driven approach to adjusting the work environment; so too is the use of a digital survey tool called Glint that professional social network LinkedIn uses to collects data on how its employees work.

GIVEN THEIR SCALE AND RESOURCES with real-estate teams and armies of consultants, one might have expected the largest firms to have the easiest time figuring out a new hybrid model and implementing a safe return to the office. That turned out not to be the case. In summer 2021, Apple CEO Tim Cook announced a new policy calling all employees back to the office on Mondays, Tuesdays and Thursdays in early autumn, only to put those plans on hold weeks later. Google, Uber and Microsoft were also forced to retreat on bringing people back. In contrast, a survey of 130 companies by real-estate advisor CBRE in summer 2021 revealed that small firms with fewer than a hundred employees were moving much faster to repopulate their offices than large ones – 80 per cent had fully reopened compared with only one-third of the largest companies.[8] Like large firms, small organizations were making crucial adjustments to their office space too, in order to meet new employee expectations and persuade people that coming back to the workplace was a good idea – even if their budgets for changes were a lot less expansive.

Across the board, we could see a new set of design and experiential values being expressed in plans to repurpose office space after the global pandemic. Unsurprisingly, making the work environment healthier was a key priority for companies keen to smooth the path to a safe office return. According to Harvard experts Joseph G. Allen and John D. Macomber, co-authors of *Healthy Buildings: How Indoor Spaces Drive Performance and Productivity* (2020), there are nine key things to consider: ventilation; air quality; thermal health; moisture; dust and pests; safety and security; water quality; noise; and lighting and views.[9]

Top of that list, given that COVID-19 emerged as an airborne pathogen, is ventilation and air quality.

In May 2021, a group of the world's leading scientists in the field called for greater regulatory stringency to control air quality in buildings, as a way of reducing the spread of COVID-19 and other illnesses. In a damning indictment of current standards, they argued that ventilation systems in office buildings today are on a par with water sanitation in the 1800s.[10] Technical initiatives around air control and filtration for offices have been a feature of workplace thinking since. However, creating the healthier office is not just about technical systems and physical health – it is also about culture and mental health. Employers focusing on their office infrastructures at the expense of the wider behavioural considerations of the workplace around psychological comfort, team identity and leadership style are unlikely to see many productivity benefits.

Linked to the healthy office is sustainability – people and planetary health are intricately tied. According to a Californian report from Next Energy Technologies, employees are not only insisting that their demands for a healthier and more sustainable work environment be taken seriously, but they're also drawing a stronger connection between the two than ever before.[11] Corporate commitment to a greener office environment stalled during the global pandemic as crisis management took priority, but real-estate developers and occupiers alike are now looking at zero carbon targets and seizing the opportunities for sustainable change – not just in new buildings but also in retrofits.

Retrofitting green features into the workplace is part of the circular economy model of 'reuse, repair and recycle'. Blackfriars Crown Court in London, for example, is being repurposed as a green commercial and community space. The scheme will create one of the largest urban roof gardens in Europe, spanning just over half a hectare (1.4 ac), with extensive access for the general public and making a significant contribution to London's ambitious targets for greening, biodiversity and sustainability.[12] The Rizzoli industrial district in Milan, meanwhile, is being revitalized with a sustainable development project called Welcome, which has been coined the 'biophilic workplace of the future'. Designed by Japanese architects Kengo Kuma and Associates, this landmark scheme anchors offices and social facilities around a newly created public piazza, with green terraces layering down to an open park.

Alongside a drive towards a more healthy and sustainable workplace, we can expect to see office space adapting to support more agile working in the hybrid model and provide more inclusive settings to meet the needs of all ages, abilities, beliefs and backgrounds. A one-size-fits-all office design was no longer relevant before COVID-19 – it is completely obsolete now. The pandemic shone a harsh glare on economic and health inequalities, placing the new onus on workplace leaders to take diversity

Roots in the Sky is a radical redevelopment of Blackfriars Crown Court in London, designed by Studio RHE. It is set to deliver one of Europe's largest urban roof gardens within a complex of work, wellness and community spaces – reimagining what an office can be.

seriously. The coronavirus crisis also pressed pause on a lot of company innovation: firms used tactical knowhow to keep operations ticking over during successive lockdowns, but genuine creativity was curbed. Now there is growing recognition among business leaders that the return to the office should bring with it a return of creative environments to foster innovation – to generate a flow of much-needed new ideas.

Making office space more supportive of creative thinking takes thoughtful design. Neuroscience research suggests that light, colour, artworks, ceiling heights, air flow and levels of comfort and interaction are all factors in stimulating innovation.[13] Curves matter too – a rounded environment is apparently more likely to enhance divergent creativity than an angular physical work environment with sharp corners. As former Bank of England chief economist Andy Haldane told the *Financial Times*: 'Exposure to new and different experiences – sounds, smells, environments, ideas, people – is a key source of creative spark.'[14]

McKinsey's London office in Holborn, designed by Morey-Smith and opened in 2021, gives some design pointers to how to make a space more creative. The traditional image of the professional service workplace, with heavy doors, closed rooms and long corridors, is transformed into a bright new destination space for 1,800 staff. To foster creativity and open collaboration with clients, McKinsey's new office is flooded with natural light and enriched with conceptual neon art. In this project, and countless others around the world, we can begin to see the design contours of the new office – repurposed space that is green, healthy, agile, inclusive, creative and blended to the hybrid mix of physical and digital work. In the wake of the COVID-19 pandemic, are we finally casting off the office-as-factory legacy of the 1920s and making the reinvention of the workplace tangible?

15 Unworking

If there were a dictionary definition of 'unworking' it would be to unravel how we work, to unbundle the assumptions that are baked into the modern office, and to unlearn the habits, management styles and workplace cultures that have traditionally defined our behaviour at work. Unworking is about reimagining and re-engineering the workplace, not simply iterating from the paper factory we know so well but taking a blank sheet of paper and starting again, free of the vestiges of our industrial past.

A new approach to defining work and workplace is needed; one that is based on the freedom to create an experience based around what people are trying to achieve. By putting people at the heart of the way we work, by recognizing their preferences and celebrating their differences, we can create a new vision for work more suited and aligned to the digital age.

We now understand that the way we work is no longer necessarily synchronous. As we've discussed, early offices were based on the production line where, by definition, everyone had to stop together to take a break. In the 9-to-5 world, people clocked in at the same time and lunch necessitated the downing of tools in a mechanized workplace where people relied on shared technology and capital.

Roll forward to today and digital disruption is having a transformative effect. Technology tools are no longer dependent on the physical office; as the cloud takes over, we are left with a thinner property that no longer has to house the infrastructure of work. The notion that work can take place from anywhere, powered by providing people with their own end-user technology tools – laptops, tablets and smartphones – means that people are now free to choose how and where they work.

'It is tough to make predictions, especially about the future,' physicist Niels Bohr is alleged to have said, and this apocryphal quote illustrates the uncertainties faced by forecasters and visionaries. But a new science of work will provide robust data sets to inform the practices that underpin unworking. No longer based on casual assumptions, groupthink, trendy design, management fads or value judgements, the new paradigm of work will have to be evidence-based; hypotheses will be tested and proved and then measured in a workplace designed by data science. Providing choice empowers people. But the concept of unworking will not leave work patterns to chance. Instead, that choice will be informed, driven by artificial intelligence and machine learning.

As the data generated by both people and buildings becomes more sophisticated, and as that data gets processed by algorithms, new insights and directions will emerge. There is now little reason to go into an office every day. Surveys conducted during the pandemic reinforced the assumption that the everyday office was becoming anachronistic. Results during lockdown showed that 45–50 per cent of people were happy to continue working from home, with the remainder mostly wanting a hybrid existence – only 5–7 per cent of people wanted to go back to the workplace as it was before lockdown.

These figures correlate to findings by Gallup, the research house, which conducts a regular survey of engagement among white-collar workers. In summer 2020, Gallup found on average that only one-third of workers (32 per cent) in the United States were 'engaged' – defined by those who are highly involved in, enthusiastic about and committed to their work and workplace.[1] More than half (54 per cent) were classified as 'not engaged' – meaning that they are psychologically unattached to their work and company. These employees 'put time, but not energy or passion into their work'. The remainder, around 14 per cent, were 'actively disengaged' – defined as those who had miserable work experiences and spread their unhappiness to their colleagues.

If only one-third of workers want to be at work, it signals a real problem with workplace culture and design. As we have described, we believe the roots lie in the repetitive monotony of the office experience today, a legacy of Taylorist efficiency that has been so hard to shake. Unworking means making the office more attractive, it needs 'pulling power' – you can mandate that people turn up, but if they don't really want to be there, productivity will be low. And just because they are at their desk, it doesn't mean they are working. So, we predict that a creative desire to design in the 'wow factor' will be accompanied by calculus models based on outputs and results, measured and driven by data. Many managers don't know how to operate in a results-driven environment; it's much easier to assemble your team and simply assert your credentials by commanding fiefdoms in the office.

The secret of unworking is to make the office one of a range of places in which work can get done, and to use apps and artificial intelligence to drive when and why people come into the office. People should be given a stipend – an annual budget for provisioning work. And they should be free to spend it as they wish within guidelines – in the corporate centre or one of its facilities or in myriad new flexible workspaces and destinations. An organization's internal facilities team will have to up its game and compete with others to attract employees.

ONE OF THE downsides of the slow death of the corporate office is the traditional methods of training people in new skills. Typically, employees learn by working alongside more senior, experienced people. They have formal training and mentoring as well as informal learning, often through osmosis and the open plan 'eavesdropping' that transfers tacit knowledge. The 'resolute returners' to the office haven't worked out how to replace this. There will be two key challenges in a digital workplace: social capital and cultural capital. The formation of networks, of reputation and trust is central to professional development – how will this social capital be built without a predictable everyday office population? And how can people learn and develop their skills without watching others and listening to their conversations – the cultural capital that can't easily be replaced by virtual places?

The workplace of tomorrow will need to replace and replicate learning and development through new formats, as advocated by the 'choice champions'. Gen Z workers already consume knowledge and develop new skills through digital platforms such as YouTube. Education was already au fait with the concept of MOOCs – massive open online courses – before experimenting with online learning during the pandemic when millions of children and students were confined to their homes. These platforms can replace formal face-to-face classroom learning, but what of the informal, unplanned and serendipitous exchanges in the office?

As part of unworking, we have developed the idea of the '6 Cs' to describe different work patterns: communication and collaboration that generate energy and velocity; concentration and contemplation that instil quality and depth; the fifth 'C', which is community, and the sixth 'C', which describes the clusters within which these activities take place. These groups are based on organizational network analysis that uses data to determine who should be with whom. And it is here that ad hoc learning can be achieved – driving people into contact when there is a new purpose, a new project, a new case or engagement or the outcome of research and development.

The hybrid office draws a line across this template to demarcate the activities that will be done from home and those that will be best accommodated by the new workplace. The calculation is based on two factors – an agility index that measures how mobile or place-independent people are in their job roles or typologies and a work from home (WFH) index that describes their hybrid workstyle based on the number of days that they will spend in the office during an average week. This 'degree of hybridity' informs not just how the organization will function but describes the requirements for workspace, the quantum of office space needed and the third spaces that will complete the vision of work spheres – the places in which work gets done in a hybrid model.

What is clear is that it is not a static equation. Needs and demands will flux and change, either through the cyclical nature of work (for example business planning or compensation and reward reviews) or the formation of teams for projects, engagements or other temporary events. Hybrid work injects uncertainty into the once predictable corporate workplace, which has to adjust, predict and become malleable.

This points to two typologies for a workplace in the future. The first is the 'elastic workplace', where a completely fluid or liquid space evolves and revolves around the work that needs to be done. Always in flux or motion, this space needs a container

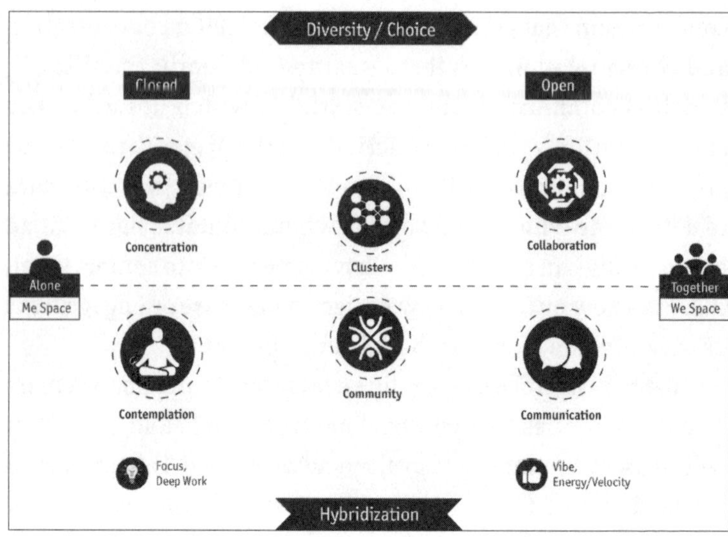

The 6 Cs model for hybrid work. UnWork (2021).

that is adaptable and flexible. The idea of the 'superflux' workplace borrows its vision from Brownian motion in chemistry, where numerous objects are in continuous motion and interaction. The *raison d'être* of the 'place of work' will more and more be around interaction and less about solo, solitary work; buildings will become physical incarnations of social networks. The other type of workplace is a team-based workplace espoused by the principles of Agile, Scrum and Kanban – defined processes and discrete teams that come together to solve problems or develop a solution. Originating in the lean manufacturing revolution pioneered by Toyota, these processes have been adopted by the software development teams that now race in sprints to launch new variants of the apps and platforms we use every day.

As we noted earlier, the experience of Gen Z today and their digital lifestyle informs much of what is to come. Their approach to real-time interaction through platforms from Snapchat to Fortnite demonstrate an expectation of being connected, always on, interacting synchronously and transparently with their friends. We have called Gen Z the 'Jelly Bean Generation' as they seem to share a 'transparency' with their friends, ranging from their location and activity to their thoughts, preferences and ideas. The Jelly Bean builds on the idea that with new digital platforms, ranging from WhatsApp to Snapchat, Microsoft Teams to Google Hangouts, people's presence is shared – their availability or state is becoming common currency. We call people's presence icon their 'Jelly Bean'.

This will have a profound impact on how we will choose to communicate, interact and work. Before the Jelly Bean, messages were asynchronous. You sent a letter but had no idea if the recipient received it or when they would reply. The telephone changed communication to become synchronous, but only if the other party was available. Now, platforms share people's status in real time. You can tell if a message has been read (and ignored) and you can see if someone is available for a chat; the Jelly Bean will be all-pervasive and challenge how and when we interact.

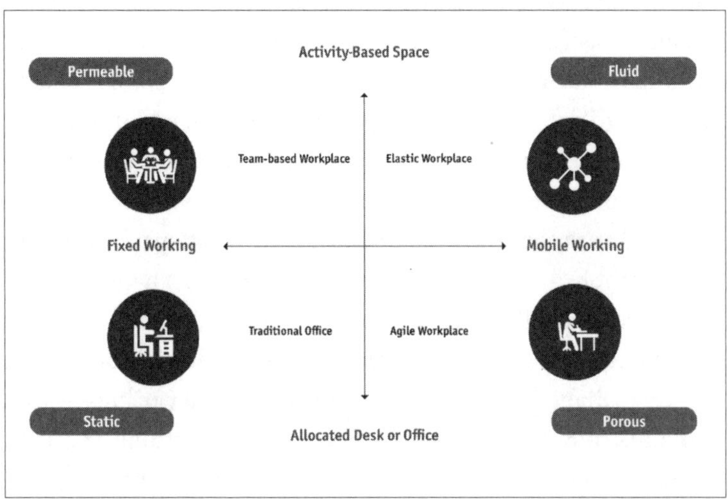

Hybrid working demands a shift from allocated desks to activity-based space. UnWork (2021).

The experience of gaming on platforms such as Fortnite and popular apps such as Uber, Amazon or Tripadvisor show that we expect interaction, personalization, localization and feedback – ratings or gamification to share or provide reviews and advice. A gamified workplace will be one consequence of the 'Xbox generation'. Gaming has become a team endeavour, a social sport, using platforms to socialize as well as to compete to win. With Snapchat, the experience of instant gratification through an exchange of visual messages that evaporate presents a vision of a different world of work; one that is in stark contrast to the staccato exchange of asynchronous communications in the form of email and text messaging developed and adopted by the Baby Boomers and Gen X. Their way of working in largely offline, scripted workplaces, with days full of back-to-back meetings in conference rooms, will be a relic of the past.

TODAY THERE IS an ability for the user to choose. But decisions and information are imperfect. And data scarcity leads to unintended consequences from ill-informed decisions – we are not optimizing our work-life integration. With AI and the use of data analytics to define an optimal working day, we will move from self-service to suggestion. An app-based experience will analyse past performance, look at current activities, review the 'data lake' and recommend where to work, in what space and with which people.

Workdays will also become more human. As we realize that the sedentary state of the office causes health impacts from obesity to diabetes, we will move towards a 'well workplace' that responds to our biorhythms and circadian rhythms to create responsive environments. Settings rich in biophilic design to provide a sense of nature, from sunlight and fresh air to scent stimuli, will be features of a great place to work. Mindfulness and 'headspace' activities will find their way in to break up the process-driven office.

People will be encouraged and empowered to manage their health. We predict the emergence of the 'quantified self' as part of workplace performance measurement – a combination of environmental data and personal metrics gathered through wearable devices, sensors and surveys. Just as athletes have their performance measured and optimized, so too can office workers. Their health will be a key factor in the design of the future workplace. As we described, sentience (how we feel) will become a key contributor to well-being measurement; data collected will reflect individual performance and result in a more personalized workplace experience.

The corporate athlete will borrow from the data science of sport and adopt a vision of margin gain – an approach that focuses on each small step towards better outcomes for both people and their place of work. As Matthew Syed describes in his book *Black Box Thinking*, learning from mistakes becomes a crucial differentiator as companies absorb lessons as opposed to burying their head in the sand. He describes how failure drives innovation and reflects on the importance of space:

> this helps to explain why cities are so creative, why atriums are important; in fact why any environment which allows disparate people, and therefore ideas, to bump into each other, is so conducive. They facilitate the association of diverse ideas, and bring people face to face with dissent and criticism. All help to ignite creativity.[2]

Divergent thinking must be encouraged, to counter groupthink. Just as other industries use intensive data to perfect performance, so the workplace will follow suit. In Formula One, for example, thousands of live data points on both the driver's and car's performances are streamed live to support teams who focus on small improvements. This approach to 'marginal gain' allows a performance enhancement that steps up in increments rather than looking or waiting for the 'big bang'. This fine-tuning is the key to creating a high-performing workplace. AI will profile workplace behaviours and guide performance through real-time insights beyond the current realms of human endeavour.

There is much talk about the rise of robots and the threat of automation and artificial intelligence to traditional employment in many sectors, as we discussed earlier. Blue-collar workers gave way to white-collar employees, who moved off the shop floor into offices (where their collars stayed clean) in the last industrial revolution; now we are heading to a 'no collar' digital workplace where 'tech turks' will fulfil tasks in a precarious gig economy. Is this just the inevitable march of technological 'progress', or should we be concerned about the dignity of work as RSA chief executive Matthew Taylor, who advised the British government on the gig economy, advocated in 'Good Work: The Taylor Review of Modern Working Practices' (2017), where he argued for 'the vital importance of good work to social justice, economic dynamism and civic engagement'.[3]

Mark Carney, the former governor of the Bank of England, warned that 'longer lives and rapid advances in technology could mean that some workers never have the option of retiring'. Britain was on the verge of entering a fourth industrial revolution that would be dominated by artificial intelligence, automation, biotechnology and 3D printing: 'The nature of work was shifting so rapidly that there was a risk that many workers would not be able to move seamlessly to new jobs, yet many may not be able to afford to retire either.'[4] Rather than fight for the jobs that will be replaced by machines, we need to identify those that won't and, more importantly, the new roles and functions yet to be created. As the Institute for the Future predicted, we are training students today for jobs that don't yet exist.

Constant change is the new reality. And so the predictions we offer here need to be embraced by a culture of open innovation that stimulates the ideas for tomorrow. This is the key challenge – creating a more fluid way of working that can flux and change with ease, rather than the rigid, structural approaches that burden us today. We will witness the transition from a workplace that is user-centred to one that is user-predicted. Just as an understanding of evolution and biology grew though testing and iteration – the continuous improvement of mankind – so the workplace should learn from evolutionary failure. The culture of 'fail fast' engrained into the Silicon Valley psyche illustrates the mantra that failure is good and should be celebrated, for that is how we learn. Failure never dared utter its name in the traditional modern office.

Principles such as these compel us to think about a new topology for office space – a building form that provides 'loose fit' and flexibility, a 'container in which people want to be' – leading to a new vision for hybrid and blended real-estate development. As we have discussed, property has historically been separated into discrete typologies and planners have kept them apart – classifications for offices, shops, residential, medical and leisure are all different. They are often located in different parts of towns and cities, and even separated out in the same economic development plans. Mixed-use developments exist but little or nothing is really shared, least of all data. These segregations fly in the face of broader socio-economic trends and the forces that are reshaping the world of work, and will be a thing of the past in the era of the intermixed digital district, as we explained in Chapter Twelve.

Transport planners have always correlated economic growth with transport growth where demand increased in line with historic data – the rush hour was never questioned and so we invested in more capacity through longer trains and platforms and new infrastructure. But as investment in moving people was committed, so people chose to move in different ways and at different times as the post-pandemic landscape became clear. Rather than succumb to traditional patterns of work in the city, a new paradigm has emerged where commuting is no longer five days a week or at predictable peaks – rush hours have been staggered, and season ticket pricing has adapted to new working patterns.

Blended use envisions an office building that is also a place where people can live and enjoy leisure, where the sharing of resources and specialist space aligns with a vision for the circular economy. Amenities such as a commercial kitchen, used during the day to deliver meals for employees or visitors, could become a dark kitchen fulfilling takeaway meals for home delivery by night. An auditorium used by day for 'town hall' meetings and corporate gatherings could become a cinema for residents in the evening. Training rooms can become classrooms, cowork spaces morph into social spaces, and company gyms and leisure facilities can be utilized 24/7. Assets can be sweated and made more effective in the shared economy. This approach would activate the city. No longer would a central business district die at the weekend. And different demographic groups could enjoy the vitality of the city – both the twenty-somethings looking for social life and the 'new silvers' with their empty nests seeking culture and buzz.

WHAT MAKES PEOPLE happy? Gallup's depressing findings assert that it is not the office or the commute. Oxytocin can perhaps help us define the science of happiness. As the hormone that is released when people bond together, it provides an analogy to the biology of the design of the right habitat for work. There is increasing evidence about the link between our physiognomy and performance. What makes us engaged or content at work? In terms of the human being, our vagus nerve has both parasympathetic nerves that control 'being' and sympathetic nerves that control activity, or 'doing'. It helps with both calmness and stress where, for example, adrenaline is triggered by deadlines, performance reviews or other pressured work activities. How can we identify and manage our physiognomy?

We are influenced by a range of factors, from environmental concerns such as air quality or light colour and temperature to pace and speed. Some environments such as trading floors or sales teams are necessarily high-pressure, compressed spaces. Do we need spaces to counter-balance, to renew and refresh, rest and recuperate? What is clear is that there is no panacea, no silver bullet, no prescriptive approach that defines the future of work. But there are clear signposts towards a different vision. We can adopt a heuristic approach to give us an outcome but increasingly we will use data to define the optimal workplace and pattern of work.

We need a more humanized workplace, so that it becomes a place where people feel they belong. In 2008, environmental psychologist Jacqueline Vischer presented a model for workplace comfort in which she described three levels: physical comfort, which provides the basic threshold of habitability; functional comfort, which adapts environmental conditions to the requirements of work; and psychological comfort, which addresses psycho-social needs such as territory, identity, well-being and belonging.[5] Psychological comfort is right at the top of the pyramid of needs in the office, and its time has come. As work becomes more atomized, the organization needs a home with a strong sense of identity.

A new workplace taxonomy will define the different ingredients that comprise the whole – a 'kit of parts' that provides the flexibility and diversity in the workplace based on the actual activities and tasks people are there to undertake. Creativity and expression will be part of a heterogeneous approach that provides choice. People should be able to adapt and adjust their environment with ease. The journey that people make through buildings should be mapped out and optimized. In *Moments of Truth* by Scandinavian Airline Systems CEO Jan Carlzon, the man behind the Frösundavik campus described in Chapter Two, he defines the opportunity to create touch points and memorable episodes. These touchpoints then define people's journeys – they form a set of experience maps that describe an individual's working day – the way that it is managed, the micro-scenarios encountered and the impression they leave. It is in our gift to shape and then manage these experiences; to optimize someone's journey so that they have a 'great day at work'. With hybrid work driving less frequent attendance at the office, we need to curate exceptional experiences to get the most out of limited moments.

Workspace design could be better aligned with retail, leisure, culture and arts at concept stage to refine the user experience; people could be focused on memorable moments, the 'wow factor' and the 'sense of awe' or wonder discussed in Chapter Four. We've entered the age of the 'Insta' (Instagram) workplace – from ice-cream parlours in the reception at Unilever Singapore or Microsoft Munich to outdoor nature pods on the green Enjoy-Work campus of Richard Rogers's Chiswick Park in London and Amazon's biospheres in Seattle.

THIS BOOK HAS described the need to bust silos to get companies in shape for the digital economy – a new corporate anthropology that describes a different realization for work and workstyle, where both sustained and disruptive innovation can thrive, where both linear and non-linear thinking can co-exist. As Andy Law of St Luke's noted, 'Changing the way you work will change the way you think.' Cognitive dissonance requires a workplace that is not in harmony. The idea of creating an atmosphere for constructive conflict and debate, for bringing disharmony into an otherwise homogenous office, will provoke the kind of discussions and generate the new ideas required for innovation. Diversity of spaces can trigger a diversity of behaviours and responses.

The consequences of digital disruption are profound. Only those organizations that embrace and become fluent in digital will survive. As the saying goes, companies will be digital predators or digital prey. 'Out of Office' was predicted to be the inevitable consequence of the rise of technology, but we have seen that people have a powerful need to get together to solve problems as well as socialize. Face to face and side by side will become prerequisites for companies that want to innovate and one of the driving forces for coming into the office.

Pre-pandemic, the polar extremes of the office and the home as the main choices for work were transformed by the growth of coworking, a broad term we discussed in Chapter Five that defines a new model for shared and flexible workspace solutions. Key to the emergence of the genre has been the adoption of a membership model and facilitated experience that centres on service with 'community hosts', coffee and beer on tap, and an activated environment that combines cool design with activity and energy. Coworking spaces provide the type of different user experience that is hard to emulate in the corporate workplace, even though big organizations are trying.

We predict the emergence of more specialized coworking spaces, modelled on the historic medieval guilds that created the first shared buildings so that people can join like-minded

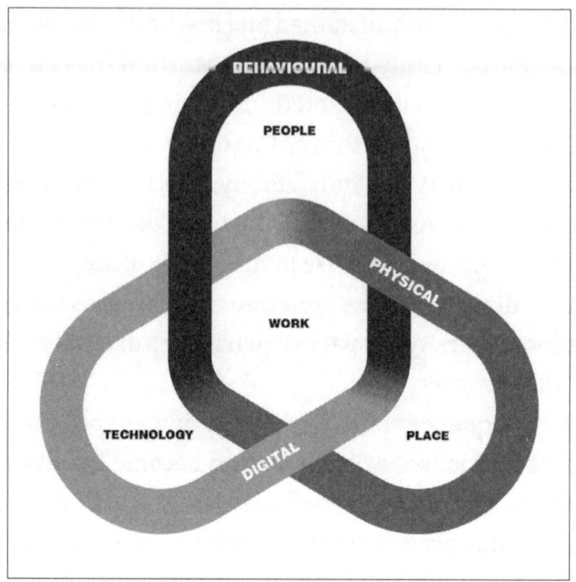

The future of work combines the behavioural, digital and physical as part of one continuum. Worktech Academy (2021).

communities based around a particular skill, craft or interest. Other formats such as The Ned in the City of London, Soho Works and No18, founded in Stockholm, are membership clubs which bring the classic 'gentlemen's club' into a twenty-first-century context where women and men share places people really want to be. Coworking allows people from different employers to share the same workspace, providing effective environments for agile workers. Boundaries will blur as hotels and office landlords provide their own version of coworking alongside service providers such as WeWork, Spaces, Industrious or The Office Group.

In the post-pandemic world, the office will shift away from one-size-fits-all to a more heterogeneous approach that celebrates diversity and is part of a digital strategy that enables a work-anywhere approach. With data and machine learning, overlaid with artificial intelligence, a new era of sophisticated planning and management will emerge. A combined approach between

HR, IT and facilities will be fundamental. As silos dissolve, so a continuum under a new unified directorate will emerge where people, place and technology are in continual flux; this directorate will set the strategy that defines the digital, physical and behavioural spheres of influence responsible for the success of any organization.

COVID-19 has fundamentally changed our assumptions about work and the workplace. Where previously there were concerns about the feasibility for people to work remotely, from home or other locations, the experiment through forced lockdowns has assuaged any lingering doubts. The ten forces described in this book have charted a new course for the office, based on a fundamental reappraisal of the nature of work and the expectations of those undertaking it. Like all journeys, it is not without its dangers and dissenters. But to realize a vision based on unworking, we believe there are ten new directions for the workplace:

1. The Social Workplace

Our research during the pandemic revealed that the number-one missing ingredient while people were working from home was socialization with colleagues. Employees missed the informal banter, the chats and catch-ups that make work human. The workplace should become a place for people and provide the experiences we need. Spaces should be designed to connect people and to accelerate and engineer serendipity. Food and drink should take centre stage as the means by which to encourage attendance and interaction. There are clubs in London today where people dine at long tables without gaps, thus creating diverse conversations between people who might not normally meet. The same applies at the university refectories where academics from different faculties discuss concepts over dinner. The curation of a social workplace through food and drink can impact both physical and cognitive performance, enable the generation of ideas and drive purpose for coming into the office.

2. The Healthy Workplace

People will want to feel good when they come into work; perhaps they should aspire to leave at the end of the day healthier than when they arrived. There are a range of contributors to health and well-being, as we discussed in Chapter Eleven, and these can be optimized. For example, people need to move around during the day; the sedentary workplace must give way to one that encourages walking, standing and circulation, where people can 'think on their feet' – literally. A healthy workplace is also a sustainable one. You cannot have a healthy workplace on a sick planet, so the future of work will place close attention to climate change; organizations will make constant efforts to reduce their environmental impact through circular economy, net zero and other initiatives.

3. The Sentient Workplace

Sentience can be enriched by both the environment – biophilia or nature, sunshine, fresh air, lighting and acoustics – and the experience at work. The way we prescribe our surroundings and conditions impact our sentience. We should consciously shape sentience, accepting that our feelings change in a cycle, driven by events ranging from business to circadian rhythms or seasonal fluctuations.

4. The Purposeful Workplace

Not only should workspace be tailored to the activities and tasks people are there to undertake, it should recognize difference and celebrate diversity: a heterogeneous workplace that aligns with individual need and provides meaning and purpose. As the pandemic exposed, people wanted to go to the office on a more occasional basis for specific tasks, and in doing so achieve more each day than simply work. People should have access to a range of amenities, whether through concierge-style services (from technology support or dry cleaning to bicycle maintenance) or new skills (professional or educational) or exercise and well-being (from gym classes or meditation to nutrition). People need to have purpose to commute into the corporate centre. They also want to engage with the city or urban spaces around them. An activated precinct or district extends purpose beyond the corporate realm.

5. The Elastic Workplace

The physical workplace has always been constrained by its inherent inflexibility. We need to model the new office on other typologies that are constantly in flux – the dynamic exhibition centre or the repertory theatre with its stage sets. We need new approaches that can embrace flex and change. Fluid or liquid space is needed to align with an agile organization in constant flux. Managing elasticity of demand effectively is a good measure of success. Most workplaces today are inelastic – they just are too inflexible to change when another variable is introduced. The secret will be to enable the elastic workplace of tomorrow, which can change when variables, such as teams and projects or seasonal differences, alter demand.

6. The Personalized Workplace

Offices have been anonymous for too long. They have evolved to better reflect brand and culture, but they can also provide a more tailored approach. Now that we all carry personal technology that interacts with the world around us, the workplace can know who is in and where people are – the ability to personalize an experience is with us. The concept of a location layer provides the experience we want, from finding a meeting room to finding a colleague. As we have experienced on the high street, GPS and geofencing technology localizes people to specific places. With over-layering and the concept of the 'mash up', intelligence and insight is added and an experience is shaped or service delivered. Inside the office, a workplace app will deliver this personalization, shaping our working day and driving the experience of work that we want. Space can become personal, aligning itself to the approach explored in Chapter Ten.

7. The Contextualized Workplace

We can also overlay onto this data set the understanding of what people are there to do. From calendar information and a host of other data sources, a contextualized workplace will evolve – one that knows not just who you are and where you are, but what you want to do, whom you need to work with and, more importantly, your preferences – the likes and dislikes that determine whether you have a 'great day at work'. Aligning space and technology with what we want to do, what we need to understand or whom we could connect with optimizes our performance and builds on ideas such as latent memory explored in Chapter Nine.

8. The Digital Workplace

Our ability to redefine the technology needed for work allows for the creation of a new digital DNA in the workplace. The vision of end-to-end digital experiences and solutions creates a platform for everything to be connected as part of a smart-space approach built on the Internet of Things. From checking in to booking a space or resources, finding a colleague or reporting a fault, a digital twin platform will enable a seamless (and touchless) experience. People will use technology based more on what they carry rather than what is anchored down to the desk. They will connect unconsciously, through ubiquitous wireless networks, to data and software that is housed in the cloud. Buildings will have their own operating system; they will be smart, connected and real time. They will still house technology infrastructure, but it will increasingly be invisible to the user.

9. The Consumerized Workplace

The slow 'hollowing out' of technology in the office as systems and platforms head to the cloud means that the interface for work can now be from personal devices using 'virtual desktop' technology, apps and web interfaces as well as emerging interfaces such as voice, haptics and mixed reality. Gone are the days of locked-in, corporate-issued technology (usually confined to the office and anchored to the desk). The idea of 'bring your own device' (or BYOD) provides the opportunity for more aspirational technology to be used at work – a blurring between what we enjoy personally for leisure and what we need for job productivity. The emergence of choice, one of the foundations of consumerism, advances the idea of a workplace-as-a-service model where people are free to choose what suits them and what works best on any given day. This is a consumption economics approach enhanced by intuitive artificial intelligence that provides the suggestions and nudges to optimize the approach. We predict that the workplace will become gamified, and just as we rate an Uber driver or a stay on Airbnb, so we will give 'star ratings' to workspace, services and support.

10. The Shared Workplace

What is clear is that we no longer need our own desk or office. While some might still benefit from working in a private space adorned with personal artefacts that stimulate and provide comfort, others prefer the variety and choice that they experience in their home or on the high street. The themes explored in this book point to a very different vision for the workplace that aligns with broader changes in society around the sharing economy. This ethos permeates the new office landscape; a series of places that are used on an 'as needed' basis and shared between people, much like the hotel or timeshare apartment. Scarcity will propel us to use our resources more efficiently and the circular economy will come to the fore with its mantra of redesign, reuse and recycle championed by Gen Z, who are motivated by environmental activism, fairness and equality.

WE HAVE EXPLORED the forces and factors that are at work, reshaping our approach to workspace and the border changes in the landscape that define how, where and when work takes place. COVID-19 has changed the rules and driven us to accelerate the changes that were already under way. We all need to be mould-breakers to survive in the uncertainty that the pandemic has brought to the surface, as our assumptions about work are upended by the forces at play.

Unworking has to start by unbundling assumptions and unlearning the behaviours that drive us back to the familiar notion of the office. Catalysed by the pandemic, we can now devise new rules and concepts that shape the experiences that people want and that drive the purpose for coming into the modern office. Driven by digital, enabled by a workplace app that nudges and suggests, and provisioned by hybridity, our journeys will be shaped in a way that recognizes different needs and requirements.

This 'kaleidoscope' or biodiversity allows us to play the game of workplace evolution where, just like snakes and ladders, some will succeed and some will fail. But what is clear is that doing nothing is no longer an option. Large and small organizations alike will seek to achieve competitive advantage in the new office – from finding talent to reducing costs.

To borrow an analogy from software, where progression is reflected in releases, our cities, buildings and workspaces need an innate ability to reinvent and upgrade themselves. Perhaps it's time that the workplace had an operating system as well that could be rebooted and updated. Making workplaces fluid and nimble may seem counter-intuitive to our understanding of the modern office of the past hundred years. But the future workplace is no longer a building but a visionary blend of people, place and technology, working in continuous harmony, enabling people to produce their best work and feel good about doing so.

In the introduction to this book we mentioned the 'swan syndrome' of workplace change: keeping up appearances above the surface while paddling frantically below. In the aftermath of the COVID-19 pandemic, the swan is paddling faster than ever. What may appear on the surface to be a graceful glide is in fact an illusion, masking the complexity of the challenge beneath as we take the digital plunge into the era of hybrid work. We continue to be confronted by shocks to the system, from the 'Great Resignation' in the global workforce to geo-political turbulence. It is this context that compels us to unlearn everything we held as sacrosanct in the world of work. *Unworking* follows this great unlearning; it is only by stepping back that we can achieve the clarity of mind and defined purpose to imagine a new world of work – and really make it happen.

References

1 Efficiency

1 Nikil Saval, *Cubed: A Secret History of the Workplace* (New York, 2014), p. 33.
2 Ibid.
3 Adrian Forty, *Objects of Desire: Design and Society, 1750–1980* (London, 1986), p. 126.
4 Jennifer Kaufmann-Buhler, *Open Plan: A Design History of the American Office* (New York, 2021), p. 168.
5 James Woudhuysen, 'Tayloring People for Production', *Design* (August 1984), pp. 34–7.
6 Saval, *Cubed*, p. 45.
7 Quoted in Daniel Rodgers, *The Work Ethic in Industrial America, 1850–1920* (Chicago, IL, 1974), p. 53.
8 Quoted in Saval, *Cubed*, p. 5.
9 Lenin's comments on Taylorism were published in *Pravda*. Saval, *Cubed*, p. 51.
10 Le Corbusier, *Towards A New Architecture* [1923] (New York, 1946), p. 87.
11 Kaufmann-Buhler, *Open Plan*, p. 19.
12 David Tong, 'Making Offices Human', *Interior Design Reference Book*, Chartered Society of Designers (London, 1989), pp. 205–8.
13 Frank Duffy quoted in *Architectural Review* (January 1979), pp. 54–8.
14 British Council for Offices report, 'The Impact of Office Design on Business Performance' (London, 2006).

2 Community

1 Jan Carlzon quoted in 'Togetherness', SAS Frösundavik corporate brochure.

2 Adrian Forty's *Objects of Desire: Design and Society, 1750–1980* (London, 1986) explains this process in detail.

3 Jennifer Kaufmann-Buhler, *Open Plan: A Design History of the American Office* (New York, 2021), p. 16.

4 Herman Hertzberger, 'The Future of the Building "Centraal Beheer"', *Hertzberger*, www.hertzberger.nl (2016).

5 The project is written up in Jeremy Myerson, *International Interiors* (London, 1995), vol. v.

6 Franklin Becker, 'Organizational Ecology and Knowledge Networks', *California Management Review*, XLIX/2 (2007), pp. 42–61.

7 Keith Alexander and Ilfryn Price, *Managing Organizational Ecologies: Space, Management and Organization* (New York and Oxford, 2012), pp. 11–22.

8 Kevin Roose, 'Sorry, But Working from Home Is Overrated', *New York Times*, www.nytimes.com, 10 March 2020, updated 1 June 2020.

3 Network

1 Peter Drucker, 'The Next Society, A Survey of the Near Future', *The Economist* (2001).

2 T. H. Davenport, R. J. Thomas and S. Cantrell, 'The Mysterious Art and Science of Knowledge-Worker Performance', *MIT Sloan Management Review* (2002).

3 Peter Drucker, 'Knowledge Worker Productivity: The Biggest Challenge', *California Management Review*, XLI/2 (1999), pp. 79–94.

4 Jeremy Myerson and Philip Ross, *Space to Work: New Office Design* (London, 2006).

5 Imogen Privett, 'Experience Unbound: The Effects of Coworking on Workplace Design Practice', PhD thesis, Royal College of Art, 2018.

6 Gabor Nagy and Greg Lindsay, 'Why Companies Are Creating Their Own Coworking Spaces', *Harvard Business Review*, https://hbr.org, 24 September 2018.

7 A. Leclercq-Vandelannoitte and H. Isaac, 'The New Office: How Coworking Changes the Work Concept', *Journal of Business Strategy*, XXXVII/6 (2016), pp. 3–9.

8 This research model was first introduced in Jeremy Myerson and Gavin Turner, *New Workspace New Culture: Office Design as a Catalyst for Change* (Aldershot, 1998).

4 Experience

1 Joseph Heller, *Something Happened* (London, 1974), p. 33.
2 Kelly Robinson was interviewed by Philip Ross for Worktech Academy, 17 July 2020.
3 Worktech Academy/Mirvac report, 'The Super Experience: Designing for Talent in the Digital Workplace' (2019).
4 Stuart Mangrum gave a keynote lecture at Worktech San Francisco, 30 October 2018.
5 Vladas Griskevicius, Michelle Shiota and Samantha Neufeld, 'Influence of Different Positive Emotions on Persuasion Processing: A Functional Evolutionary Approach', *Emotion*, x/2 (2010), pp. 190–206.
6 Sally Augustin, 'Awe-Inspiring Design Can Really Deliver – The Scientific Evidence', Worktech Academy, www.worktechacademy.com, 25 May 2018.
7 Deloitte Global Human Capital Trends report (2017).

5 Organization

1 General Stanley McChrystal is a regular speaker at Worktech conferences.
2 Stanley A. McChrystal, *Team of Teams: New Rules of Engagement for a Complex World* (London, 2015), p. 23.
3 Ibid.
3 Gillian Tett, *The Silo Effect: The Peril of Expertise and the Promise of Breaking Down Barriers* (London, 2014), p. 62.
4 Walter Isaacson, *Steve Jobs* (New York, 2011), p. 362.
5 Zhang Ruimin, 'Raising Haier', *Harvard Business Review*, https://hbr.org, accessed 31 August 2021.
6 Louis Sullivan, 'The Tall Office Building Artistically Considered', *Lippincott's Magazine* (1896).
7 Daniel Brosseau et al., 'The Journey to an Agile Organization', www.mckinsey.com, 10 May 2019.

6 Urbanism

1 Panel debates between city leaders and urban planners at the inaugural Healthy City Design International Congress (Royal College of Physicians, London, 2017) helped to kickstart this debate.
2 'Paris Is Planning to Become a 15-Minute City', https://fr.weforum.org, 16 July 2021.

3 Arney Fender Kasalidis/Worktech Academy report, 'The Future of Flex: Flexible Workspace in the UK Post Covid-19' (2021), www.worktechacademy.com; 'The Future of Flex: Can UK Flexible Workspace Bounce Back?', 26 July 2021.
4 Frances Cairncross interviewed by Philip Ross for Worktech Academy, 8 March 2021.

7 Space

1 Harrison Owen, *Open Space Technology* (San Francisco, CA, 2008), p. 5.
2 See https://dschool.stanford.edu, accessed 31 August 2021.
3 Jeremy Myerson, 'How People Work: Under-Utilised Space in Offices Everywhere', *Worktech Academy*, www.worktechacademy.com, accessed 31 August 2021.
4 'U.S. Workplace Survey 2020', Gensler Research Institute (2020).
5 Brodie Boland et al., 'Reimagining the Office and Work Life after Covid-19', www.mckinsey.com, 8 June 2020.
6 Philip Stone and Robert Luchetti, 'Your Office Is Where You Are', *Harvard Business Review* (1985) (March/April 1985), pp. 102–12.
7 The 2003 Interpolis is described in detail in Jeremy Myerson and Philip Ross, *Space to Work* (London, 2006).
8 Jane Croft, 'COVID-19 Reinvents Law Firm Offices as Hubs for Teamwork and Socialising', *Financial Times*, www.ft.com, 1 October 2020.
9 Klaus Sandbiller of UniCredit interviewed by Jeremy Myerson, 4 May 2021.
10 Ray Oldenburg, *Celebrating the Third Place* (New York, 2001).

8 Technology

1 This shift was predicted in Frances Cairncross, *The Death of Distance: How the Communications Revolution Will Change Our Lives* (Boston, MA, 1997).
2 Philip Ross, 'The Cordless Office' (Cordless Consultants, 1994).
3 Jimmy Stamp, 'Fact of Fiction? The Legend of the QWERTY Keyboard', *Smithsonian Magazine*, www.smithsonianmag.com, accessed 31 August 2021.
4 See the Worktech Guide to Workplace Apps, www.worktechacademy.com.
5 AXA's Goldsmith and Badham spoke about 22 Bishopsgate at a Worktech virtual event on smart buildings, 24 February 2021.

6 RSA, 'The Four Futures of Work: Coping with Uncertainty in an Age of Radical Technologies' (London, 2019), presented by Matthew Taylor at the Worktech Conference, London, 27 November 2019.

9 Designing

1 Andy Law, *Open Minds: 21st Century Business Lessons and Innovations from St Luke's* (Knutsford, 2001), p. 135. Law was a popular speaker at Worktech.
2 Ibid., p. 139.
3 Ulrich Blum of Zaha Hadid Architects spoke at Worktech Berlin, 4 July 2017.
4 Helen Hamlyn Centre for Design, Royal College of Art/Gensler research report, 'Workplace and Wellbeing' (London, 2017).
5 Ken Lynch of ANZ Bank spoke at a Worktech conference, London, November 2015.
6 Nicholas Taleb, *The Black Swan: The Impact of the Highly Improbable* (London and New York, 2007).
7 Jeremy Myerson, *IDEO: Masters of Innovation* (London, 2001), p. 30.
8 Worktech Academy/Lendlease report, 'From Desk to District: Expanding Horizons in Collaborative Innovation', www.worktechacademy.com, 2018.

10 Diversity

1 Carl Jung, *Psychological Types* (Zurich, 1927).
2 F. S. Morgenstern, R. J. Hodgson and L. Law, 'Work Efficiency and Personality: A Comparison of Introverted and Extraverted Subjects Exposed to Conditions of Distraction and Distortion of Stimulus in a Learning Task', *Ergonomics*, XVII/2 (1974), pp. 211–20.
3 Cal Newport, *Deep Work: Rules for Focused Success in a Distracted World* (London, 2016).
4 Mihaly Csikszentmihalyi, *Flow: The Psychology of Optimal Experience* (New York, 1990).
5 Susan Cain, *Quiet: The Power of Introverts in a World that Can't Stop Talking* (New York, 2012), p. 84.
6 Ibid., p. 93.
7 Ibid.
8 Alison Reynolds and David Lewis, 'Teams Solve Problems Faster When They're More Cognitively Diverse', *Harvard Business Review* (30 March 2017).
9 Edward de Bono, *Six Thinking Hats* (Harmondsworth, 1985).
10 Interview with Philip Ross, 1998.

11 Thomas Barta, Markus Kleiner and Tilo Neumann, 'Is There a Payoff From Top-Team Diversity?', www.mckinsey.com, 1 April 2012.
12 Jennifer Kaufmann-Buhler, *Open Plan: A Design History of the American Office* (New York, 2021), p. 38.
13 Ibid., p. 73.
14 Steven Johnson, *Where Good Ideas Come From: The Natural History of Innovation* (London, 2010), p. 45.
15 Ibid.
16 Newport, *Deep Work*, p. 55.
17 Kay Sargent, 'WORKTECH Webinar: Designing Smart Offices in the New Era of Work', *Unwired Venture* (2020), www.vimeo.com, accessed 1 September 2021.
18 Johnson, *Where Good Ideas Come From*, p. 55.

11 Well-Being

1 Tom Savigar speaking at Worktech's Wellness conference, 5 September 2017.
2 Jim Taylour spoke at the Worktech New York conference, 26 May 2016.
3 Nina Reece, 'Workers Say No to Increased Surveillance since COVID-19', www.tuc.org.uk, 1 March 2022.
4 Experts on this panel contributed to a Worktech Academy/ Fourfront Group report, 'The Puzzle of Wellbeing: Where Next for Workplace Wellbeing Post COVID-19?' (London, 2020).
5 Karen Jeffrey et al., 'Wellbeing at Work', New Economics Foundation, 26 March 2014.
6 Craig Knight and S. Alexander Haslem, 'The Relative Merits of Lean, Enriched, and Empowered Offices: An Experimental Examination of the Impact of Workspace Management Strategies on Well-Being and Productivity', *Journal of Experimental Psychology Applied*, XVI/2 (June 2010), pp. 158–72.
7 Mohammad Mahdi Foroudi et al., 'Explicating Place Identity Attitudes, Place Architecture Attitudes, and Identification Triad Theory', *Journal of Business Research*, CVIX (2020), pp. 321–36.
8 'Productivity, Technology and Working Anywhere', Lancaster University Management School (2018).
9 Worktech Academy, 'Executives and Employees at Odds Over New World of Work', www.worktechacademy.com, 14 October 2020.
10 Martec, 'Amid Pandemic, New and Unique Employee Segments Emerge in Response to Remote Working Conditions', https://martecgroup.com, accessed 1 September 2021.

11 Dr Fiona Kerr spoke at Worktech's Workplace Innovation virtual conference, 26 March 2021.

12 Hybridity

1 Worktech Academy/Mirvac report, 'The Future of the Smart Precinct: A Physical-Digital Intermix for City Innovation', www.worktechacademy.com (2019).
2 Jeremy Myerson and Klaus Sandbiller, 'Hybrid Space Making: Rethinking the Bank Branch Experience for the Digital Age', *Corporate Real Estate Journal*, VII/3 (Spring 2018), pp. 256–66.
3 Ibid.
4 See Jeremy Myerson and Imogen Privett, 'Emotional Landscapes', in *Life of Work: What Office Design Can Learn from the World Around Us* (London, 2014), pp. 42–69.
5 Ibid.
6 Kevin McCullagh, 'Robot Reboot: Why We Should Stop Taking Fright at Automation', Worktech Academy, www.worktechacademy.com, 22 February 2019.
7 Worktech Academy/Mirvac report, 'Augmented Work: How New Technologies are Reshaping the Global Workplace', www.worktechacademy.com (2020).

13 Demography

1 Workforce Institute report on Gen Z, see Dana Wilkie, 'Generation Z Says They Work the Hardest, But Only When They Want To', www.shrm.org, 11 June 2019.
2 Logitech, 'Why Video-First Organisations Will Win Over Generation Z', Worktech Academy, www.worktechacademy.com, 30 January 2020.
3 Milken Institute and Stanford Center for Longevity, 'The Power of an Older Workforce', www.linkedin.com (2016).
4 Daron Acemoglu and Pascual Restrepo, 'Robots and Jobs: Evidence from U.S. Labor Markets', *Journal of Political Economy*, CXXVIII/6 (June 2020), pp. 2188–244.
5 Lynda Gratton and Andrew Scott, *The 100-Year Life: Living and Working in an Age of Longevity* (London, 2016).
6 Lynda Gratton and Andrew Scott, *The New Long Life: A Framework for Flourishing in a Changing World* (London, 2020).
7 Lynda Gratton spoke at Worktech Tokyo 2020.
8 Robert Morison, Tamara Erickson and Ken Dychtwald, 'Managing Middlescence', *Harvard Business Review* (March 2006).

9 Rich Cohen, 'Why Generation X Might Be Our Last, Best Hope', *Vanity Fair* (11 August 2017), www.vanityfair.com, accessed 1 September 2021.
10 Aramark/Worktech Academy, 'Industry Insights: What Makes A Great Workplace?' (San Francisco, CA, 2019).
11 Jeremy Myerson and Jo-Anne Bichard, 'Welcoming Workplace: Rapid Design Intervention to Determine the Office Environment Needs of Older Knowledge Workers', in *Design for the 21st Century*, vol. II: *Interdisciplinary Methods and Findings*, ed. T. Inns (Farnham, 2009).
12 Ethan S. Bernstein and Stephen Turban, 'The Impact of the "Open" Workspace on Human Collaboration', *Philosophical Transactions of the Royal Society B: Biological Sciences*, CCCLXXIII/1753 (2018).
13 Journalist Dan Lyons describes how he tried and failed to make a duck out of Lego bricks in *Lab Rats: Tech Gurus, Junk Science, and Management Fads – My Quest to Make Work Less Miserable* (New York, 2019), p. 8.
14 Ibid.
15 Lucy Kellaway, 'Apple Has Built an Office for Grown-Ups', *Financial Times*, www.ft.com, 2 July 2017.

14 Repurposing

1 Robert Glazer, 'The CEO of Goldman Sachs Called Remote Working an Aberration – Here's Why His Employees May Disagree', *Forbes Magazine*, www.forbes.com, 11 May 2021.
2 Laura Noonan, 'Citi's Next CEO Jane Fraser on Regulators, Covid and Breaking the Gender Barrier', *Financial Times*, www.ft.com, 2 December 2020.
3 Paul Clarke, 'How Are You Going to Learn Properly?: JPMorgan CEO Jamie Dimon Warns of Increasing Negative of Working from Home', *Financial News*, www.fnlondon.com, 16 October 2020.
4 Microsoft, 'The Next Great Disruption Is Hybrid Work – Are We Ready?', www.microsoft.com, 22 March 2021.
5 Kari Paul, 'Salesforce Shifts Away from In-Person Work: "The 9–5 Workday Is Dead"', *The Guardian*, www.theguardian.com, 10 February 2021.
6 Worktech Academy/Mirvac report, 'From Office to Omni-Channel: The Rise of the Omni-Channel Worker in the Digital Age' (2020).
7 Kalyeena Makortoff, 'Lloyds Embraces Hybrid Working with 20% Cut in Office Space', *The Guardian*, www.theguardian.com, 24 February 2021.

8 'How Are Office Occupiers Planning for the Future?', CBRE, August 2021, referenced in 'The Great Resignation: Why are Knowledge Workers Quitting En Masse?', Worktech Academy, www.worktechacademy.com, 26 August 2021.
9 Joseph G. Allen and John D. Macomber, *Healthy Buildings: How Indoor Spaces Drive Performance and Productivity* (Cambridge, MA, 2020).
10 L. Morawska et al., 'A Paradigm Shift to Combat Indoor Respiratory Infection', *Science*, CCCLXXII/6543 (May 2021), pp. 689–91.
11 NEXT Energy Report, 'The Case For Office Space: How Buildings Need to Change to Suit a Climate-Conscious, Covid-Weary Workforce', www.nextenergytech.com, 1 July 2021.
12 Matilde Moro, 'Roots in the Sky – London Will See Its First Rooftop Forest in 2024', *Lampoon Magazine*, www.lampoonmagazine.com, 5 August 2021. See also New London Architecture report, 'WRK/LDN: Office Revolution?', https://nla.london, 19 May 2021.
13 Sally Augustin, 'The Big Design Moves That Can Boost Creativity at Work', Worktech Academy, www.worktechacademy.com, 21 June 2021.
14 Quoted in Emma Jacobs, 'Where's the Spark? How Lockdown Caused a Creativity Crisis', *Financial Times*, www.ft.com, 18 January 2021.

15 Unworking

1 Jim Harter, 'Historic Drop in Employee Engagement Follows Record Rise', www.gallup.com, 2 July 2020.
2 Matthew Syed, *Black Box Thinking* (London, 2015), p. 215.
3 Matthew Taylor, 'Good Work: The Taylor Review of Modern Working Practices', RSA publication (July 2017), www.thersa.org.
4 Mark Carney was quoted in Peter O'Dwyer, 'Workers May Lose Option of Retiring, Says Mark Carney', *The Times*, www.thetimes.co.uk, 15 September 2018.
5 Jacqueline Vischer, 'Towards an Environmental Psychology of Workspace: How People are Affected by Environments for Work', *Architectural Science Review*, LI/2 (June 2008), pp. 97–108.

Select Bibliography

Alexander, Keith, and Ilfryn Price, *Managing Organizational Ecologies: Space, Management and Organization* (New York and Oxford, 2012)

Allen, Joseph, and John Macomber, *Healthy Buildings: How Indoor Spaces Drive Performance and Productivity* (Cambridge, MA, 2020)

Brand, Stewart, *How Buildings Learn* (London, 1994)

Brown, Tim, *Change by Design: How Design Thinking Transforms Organizations and Inspires Innovation* (New York, 2009)

Cain, Susan, *Quiet: The Power of Introverts in a World that Can't Stop Talking* (New York, 2012)

Cairncross, Frances, *The Death of Distance: How the Communications Revolution Will Change Our Lives* (Boston, MA, 1997)

Clements-Croome, Derek, ed., *Creating the Productive Workplace: Places to Work Creatively*, 3rd edn (London and New York, 2018)

Csikszentmihalyi, Mihaly, *Flow: The Psychology of Optimal Experience* (New York, 1990)

De Bono, Edward, *Six Thinking Hats* (Harmondsworth, 1985)

Duffy, Francis, *The New Office* (London, 1997)

—, *Work and the City* (London, 2008)

—, et al., *Design for Change: The Architecture of DEGW* (Basel, Boston, MA, and Berlin, 1998)

Forty, Adrian, *Objects of Desire: Design and Society, 1750–1980* (London, 1986)

Gillen, Nicola, *Future Office: Next-Generation Workplace Design* (London, 2019)

Graf Klein, Judy, *The Office Book* (London, 1982)

Gratton, Lynda, and Andrew Scott, *The 100-Year Life: Living and Working in an Age of Longevity* (London, 2016)

—, *The New Long Life: A Framework for Flourishing in a Changing World* (London, 2020)

Groves, Kursty, *I Wish I Worked There!* (Hoboken, NJ, 2010)

—, and Oliver Marlow, *Spaces for Innovation: The Design and Science of Inspiring Environments* (Amsterdam, 2016)

Handy, Charles, *The Empty Raincoat: Making Sense of the Future* (London, 1994)

—, *Gods of Management: The Changing Work of Organizations* (Oxford, 1996)

Heller, Joseph, *Something Happened* (London, 1974)

Hofstede, Geert, *Culture's Consequences: Comparing Values, Behaviors, Institutions and Organizations Across Nations* (Thousand Oaks, CA, and London, 2003)

Hsieh, Tony, *Delivering Happiness: A Path to Profits, Passion, and Purpose* (New York, 2010)

Isaacson, Walter, *Steve Jobs* (New York, 2011)

Jacobs, Jane, *The Death and Life of Great American Cities* (New York, 1961)

Johnson, Steven, *Where Good Ideas Come From: The Natural History of Innovation* (London, 2010)

Jung, Carl, *Psychological Types* (Zurich, 1921)

Kane, Chris, *Where Is My Office? Reimagining the Workplace for the 21st Century* (London, 2020)

Kaufmann-Buhler, Jennifer, *Open Plan: A Design History of the American Office* (New York, 2021)

Law, Andy, *Open Minds: 21st Century Business Lessons and Innovations from St Luke's* (London, 1999)

Le Corbusier, *Towards A New Architecture* (New York, 1946)

Leigh, Alan, and David Firth, *The Corporate Fool* (Oxford, 1998)

Lyons, Dan, *Lab Rats: Tech Gurus, Junk Science, and Management Fads: My Quest to Make Work Less Miserable* (New York, 2019)

McChrystal, Stanley A., *Team of Teams: New Rules of Engagement for a Complex World* (London, 2015)

Myerson, Jeremy, and Imogen Privett, *Life of Work: What Office Design Can Learn from the World Around Us* (London, 2014)

—, and Emily Gee, eds, *Time and Motion: Redefining Working Life* (Liverpool, 2013)

—, Jo-Anne Bichard and Alma Erlich, *New Demographics, New Workspace: Office Design for the Changing Workforce* (Farnham, 2010)
—, and Philip Ross, *The Creative Office* (London, 1999)
—, and —, *The 21st Century Office* (London, 2003)
—, and —, *Space to Work: New Office Design* (London, 2006)
—, and Gavin Turner, *New Workspace New Culture: Office Design as a Catalyst for Change* (Aldershot, 1998)
Newport, Cal, *Deep Work: Rules for Focused Success in a Distracted World* (London, 2016)
Oldenburg, Ray, *Celebrating the Third Place* (New York, 2001)
Owen, Harrison, *Open Space Technology: A User's Guide* (San Francisco, CA, 2008)
Pélegrin-Genel, Elisabeth, *The Office* (Paris, 1996)
Rodgers, Daniel, *The Work Ethic in Industrial America, 1850–1920* (Chicago, IL, 1974)
Saval, Nikil, *Cubed: A Secret History of the Workplace* (New York, 2014)
Syed, Matthew, *Black Box Thinking* (London, 2015)
Taleb, Nicholas, *The Black Swan: The Impact of the Highly Improbable* (London and New York, 2007)
Tett, Gillian, *The Silo Effect: The Peril of Expertise and the Promise of Breaking Down Barriers* (London, 2014)
—, *Anthro-Vision: How Anthropology Can Explain Business and Life* (London, 2021)
Usher, Neil, *The Elemental Workplace* (London, 2019)

Acknowledgements

The ideas in this book have been sourced, shaped and shared through countless conversations, presentations and projects with stimulating people and adventurous companies in the Worktech community over more than twenty years. Through our global Worktech conferences and the Worktech Academy membership network, we have been privileged to collaborate with the pioneers who are creating the future of work. We've also found ourselves enriched by consulting engagements via Unwork and Cordless Consultants, and our relationships with the Helen Hamlyn Centre for Design at the Royal College of Art, London, and other research centres. Thank you to all the individuals and organizations who contributed to *Unworking* – your insights, generosity and vision made the task of writing this book that much easier. Our thanks also go to our wonderful colleagues at Unwired, and the brilliant team at Reaktion Books, who believed in this project from the start and made it happen.

Photo Acknowledgements

The authors and publishers wish to express their thanks to the below sources of illustrative material and/or permission to reproduce it. Every effort has been made to contact copyright holders; should there be any we have been unable to reach or to whom inaccurate acknowledgements have been made please contact the publishers, and full adjustments will be made to any subsequent printings:

© AHH: p. 39 (photo Willem Diepraam); Alamy Stock Photo: pp. 27 (Photo 12/United Artists), 28 (A. F. Archive), 32 (Prisma by Dukas Presseagentur GmbH, photo Frank Chmura), 46 (Alexander Cimbal), 60 (Lukas Bischoff), 76 (Chronicle), 98 (CAMimage); courtesy Bjarke Ingels Group: p. 170; courtesy Boston Consulting Group: p. 136; Clive Wilkinson Architects: pp. 42 and 43 (photos Benny Chan/Fotoworks); courtesy Comfy: p. 114; courtesy Combine Consulting: p. 36; © Ezra Stoller/Esto: p. 18; Aaron Gustafson (CC BY-SA 2.0): p. 41; courtesy Herman Miller: p. 29; iStock.com: p. 95 (ZU_09); Library of Congress, Prints and Photographs Division, Washington, DC: pp. 23, 25 (Gottscho-Schleisner Collection); courtesy Meta: p. 156; courtesy Michael Grubb Studio: p. 201; courtesy MoreySmith (photo Philip Durrant) p. 190; courtesy Micaël Queiroz: p. 93; Royal College of Art, London: pp. 168 (Andrew Thompson), 174 (Imogen Privett), 178 (Helen Hamlyn Centre for Design, photo Petr Krejci); courtesy Salesforce, San Francisco: p. 65; Shutterstock.com: p. 6 (Everett Collection); courtesy Stanford d.school, Hasso Plattner Institute of Design, Stanford University,

CA: p. 104; Unsplash: pp. 99 (Jermaine Ee), 142 (Patrick Schneider); diagrams by UnWork: pp. 208, 209; courtesy Veldhoen & Company: p. 102; Victoria and Albert Museum, London: p. 88; diagrams by Worktech Academy: pp. 50, 67 (Mirvac), 74 (after Stanley A. McChrystal, *Team of Teams: New Rules of Engagement for a Complex World* (London, 2015)), 85 (after Charles Handy, *Gods of Management: The Changing Work of Organizations* (Oxford, 1996)), 140 (Lendlease), 196 (Mirvac), 218; courtesy Zaha Hadid Architects: p. 128.

Index

Page numbers in *italics* indicate illustrations